MAKE THE RIGHT DECISIONS EARLY

MAKE THE RIGHT DECISIONS EARLY

Wisdom for Pre-College Students and Other Teens

TOM McKINLEY

MAKE THE RIGHT DECISIONS EARLY
Wisdom for Pre-College Students and Other Teens

iUniverse books may be ordered through booksellers or by contacting:

iUniverse
1663 Liberty Drive
Bloomington, IN 47403
www.iuniverse.com
1-800-Authors (1-800-288-4677)

ISBN: 978-1-5320-1458-1 (sc)
ISBN: 978-1-5320-1459-8 (e)

Library of Congress Control Number: 2017900323

Print information available on the last page.

iUniverse rev. date: 02/15/2017

Back cover photograph courtesy of Michael Burns

Table of Contents

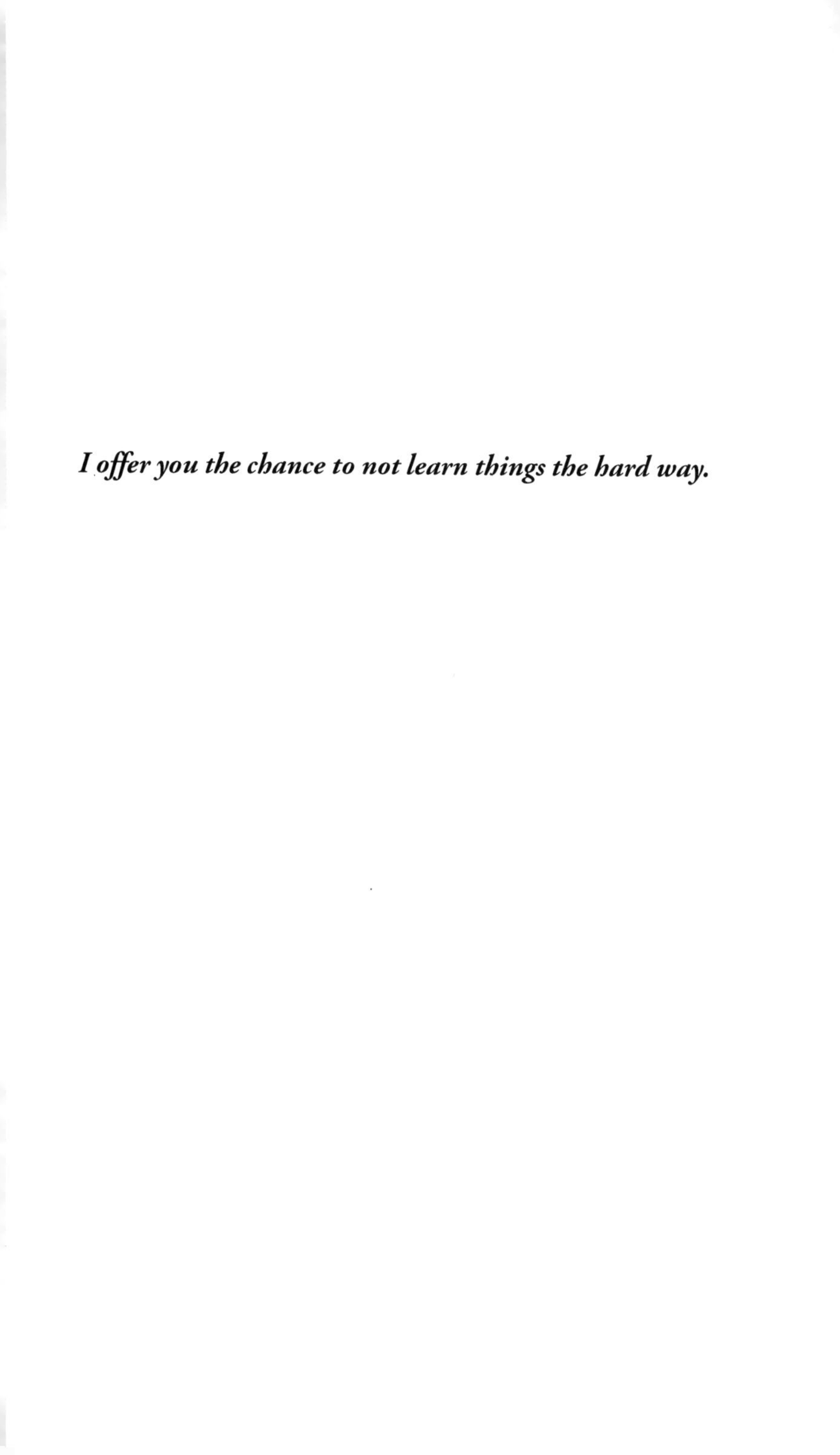

I offer you the chance to not learn things the hard way.

INTRODUCTION

My inspiration for ***Make the Right Decisions Early*** arose from observing the thousands of students who graduate from college each year. Many of them leave college with as little idea what to do with their professional lives than when they first set foot on campus four years earlier. The university system continues to present itself as a means for someone to enter the working world and succeed. Yet it fails to specifically define the role that it actually plays. While college presents itself as a guide, it is really just a tool, and one that students need to know how to use properly and to their advantage.

Graduation from college is a joy-filled day, with much celebrating, usually in the sun and among family. The next day, many students wake up to the realizations that college is *over*, and that they are not employable. Students need to be aware of this possibility before they even go to college, such that they can use those four years in a way that makes graduation day a beginning rather than an end.

The education system has circumvented the responsibility of providing students with career direction. Students do not receive sufficient career advice and guidance to make the extremely important decisions which will affect them for the rest of their lives. Such direction is not provided by colleges, as seen in the huge number of graduates who are professionally lost in the wilderness after they finish their degrees. And high schools? The main objective of high schools, in their view, is to get students into high-ranking, prestigious schools which reflect prestige onto their own institution. There is still the erroneous feeling that college will sort out the direction that students should take.

This book fills that gap in direction. I have designed it to give practical, straightforward guidance to students, such that they do not wake up on the morning after their graduation day with stress about their future and no clear idea of where to take their professional life—while being saddled with immense debt.

Certainly, life has become harder for the college graduate over the past 20 years. If you are from the middle classes, it is increasingly harder to achieve the quality of life that we have been taught to aspire to. It is also increasingly difficult to preserve the middle-class status that we have been born into. With a shrinking middle class, we have to be more strategic than ever to ensure that we have the elements that are required for a financially strong and stable future.

Make the Right Decisions Early also provides guidance to students on how to make the *personal* best use of their college years. While college is one of the few times in our lives where it is acceptable to be living with one foot in the future, there is indeed the present that one must also be concerned with. For you, the student planning to go to college—or already in your first year—this is a time in which you are still maturing in so many ways: socially, physically, cerebrally, and psychologically. It is also, ironically, a time at which you are feeling a rush of feelings of independence and hence least likely to ask for guidance.

With all this in mind, I have divided the book into two main parts. Part One focuses on direction, majors, and careers, and gives information that will enable you to take the right courses and secure a well-paying job in an upwardly-mobile career. Part Two discusses the less tangible, but still extremely important, factors in having a successful college experience—the ones that will contribute to your character at this time of life and in the prosperous and happy future which I am planning for you to have.

This book is designed to give you the best shot at making the most of these pivotal years. Like it or not, these years will impact the rest of your life.

In short, I have written it with the goal of seeing people take the right steps upon entering college, so that they can take smooth steps upon leaving it. While I encourage you to keep an open mind when you are reading, feel free to disagree with me when you want—but never forget that my goal here is to see you gliding comfortably from high school to college to the working world. I speak from experience and know that it is my duty to tell you the realities, no matter how uncomfortable they may seem. There's no reason to learn the hard way when you can learn in a way that is easy and saves you tons of time and frustration.

And so with that, let us begin on the path to seeing you as a healthy, happy, and successful college student and graduate, and a member of the working world.

PART ONE

1 Money: It's More Important than You Think

I will be giving you specific guidance on majors and careers—but first, it is necessary to give a brief lesson on money.

Money will be extremely important in your life, and anyone who tells you otherwise is either ignorant or self-deluded. High school and college both fail to illustrate the connection between *what* you study and your financial comfort in life.

We will shortly be discussing what is meant by financial comfort, but for now, I want to stress the fact that money is important psychologically, emotionally, socially, and physically. In my teens, wrapped up in the fervor of high school intellectualism, I challenged statements such as these, but as I got into my mid-20s I found that they were true. They are simple facts of life, just as true as the laws of physics and mathematics.

Unfortunately, the world is full of people who will tell you the opposite. We hear it from pop bands as well as from colleges themselves. The hippy movement, noble as it was for praising peace and equality, ultimately lost traction because it failed to acknowledge the importance of money in life, especially as its members entered their 20s. Yes, peace and love are important, but so is money. Part of our existence involves the need to survive. And money is a critical part of survival.

Part of our existence involves the need to survive. And money is a critical part of survival.

Older people will tell you that "Your health is all that matters." They are exaggerating. Yes, health is the most important thing; but is it fun to be healthy and poor? Or healthy and without direction? Don't be deceived by such absolutist descriptions of health. It is indeed important, but it's not everything.

Money, also, is certainly not everything, but at your age, beware of people who belittle its importance. Unless these people are going to take care of you financially for the rest of your life, they are actually harming you by feeding you false statements.

Hence, do not wait till your 20s to find out the hard way that money is a foundation for happiness. Money has a huge influence on our lives—much more than we can imagine as teenagers. Let's use some syllogistic reasoning here. We need money to live. And in order to make money, you need a job. If you want a fairly decent life, you need a fairly well-paying job. Aiming for an "average" income is no longer a safe option, as the average income does not enable you to comfortably afford a home or to have a lifestyle that is financially stress-free. The middle class is shrinking, but prices are not.

The Salary Threshold

In 2010, ***Time*** magazine published an article about an economic study by two Princeton professors that stated the threshold for financial comfort. The research, by Angus Deaton and Daniel Kahneman, yielded that a minimum income of $75,000 per year (for a single adult) was needed to provide a feeling of financial security.

If you earn that sum, you can have a car problem on the way to work and not stress about having to pay the money to get it fixed; your laptop can break down and need to be replaced, and it doesn't ruin your month.

For those who earn under that amount, every unexpected expense becomes a crisis. That money for the new tire or laptop comes out of your food budget, or you feel guilty putting on the heat or air-conditioning in the house because you need that money for the new laptop.

Furthermore, having the sum prescribed by Kahneman and Deaton enables us to have a disposable income, allowing us to make the occasional unnecessary purchase, go for a nice dinner, or even plan a trip to Europe.

A follow-up study in 2014, in *Business Insider*, put the figure at $83,000. This will of course have risen since 2014, and for the purposes of this book, I'll be using a figure of $88,000. (The figure is of course higher if one wants to live in extraordinarily expensive places, such as central Manhattan or San Francisco.) By the time you graduate from college, it will be well over $90,000.

Naturally, not all jobs pay $88,000 to start. But a job should have the *potential* to pay you $88,000 after five to eight years. Otherwise, you are fighting a losing battle, financially.

Bear in mind that $88,000 is not a "sweet spot," or an indication of perfect work-life balance. People earning more than $88,000 do not experience a drop in happiness, and are likely to be *happier*, as their disposable income makes it easier to do away with unpleasant things. The salary of $88,000 is rather the minimum level at which we can have some financial peace of mind and then climb upwards on the happiness ladder.

BEING KNOWLEDGEABLE ABOUT MONEY

We learn a language by trying to speak it. And money is a language.

We learn a language by trying to speak it. And money is a language.

One thing you will notice about wealthy people is that they like to talk about money. They talk about money in the same way that jocks talk about sports and geeks talk about computers. Rich families talk about money freely, but for some reason, middle-class people avoid the subject. We don't talk about it at the dinner table, and because our lives are so busy, we rarely get a chance to meet and talk about our finances at all.

A lot can be learned from your parents about money, even just how your house was financed, or what insurance you have, or any investments they are doing for themselves. Take a lesson from rich people: don't be afraid to talk about your personal financial situation. It's one of the ways that you learn. While "If you understand money, you understand the world" may be an exaggeration, money is very related to human behavior, and the economy is indeed part of our lives. It influences politics, emotions, families, lifestyles, and education, just to name a few. It's worth being knowledgeable about.

On any given day, you should know the exact sum in your bank account. If you don't know it right now, at this very moment, that is forgivable. But if you don't know it by this time tomorrow, that is your fault. The same goes for writing a check. When I finished high school, I still didn't know how to fill one out. Don't let this be you. Go straight into the other room right now and ask your mom to teach you.

On any given day, you should know the exact sum in your bank account.

In addition to your bank balance, you should know about any certificates of deposit (CDs), loans, or investments that you have, and should be familiar with all the details. This might sound boring compared to your hobbies and chatting on social media, but it is actually a lot more important. The "boring" things in life are often the things that matter most. Not surprisingly, one characteristic of CEOs is that they have a high tolerance for boredom.

The Shrinking Middle Class

As mentioned above, money will be important in your life. This may be the biggest understatement you've ever read. And hence it helps to look at the current economic situation, as there is a definite and very alarming trend. We are in the midst of a historic economic shift, which involves the shrinking of the middle class. This is due to a variety of reasons, one of which is outsourcing. Increasingly, we will see a more feudalistic system of wealthy landowners and a larger lower-income segment of the population.

Writing in 2007, Robert H. Frank, in his book ***Falling Behind: How Rising Inequality Harms the Middle Class***, stated that "Although the top 1% of earners now have more than three times as much purchasing power as in 1979, the real earnings of families in the middle have risen only slightly since then." He adds that "The meager income growth that these families have experienced has come not from hourly wage increases, but rather from growth in the labor force participation of married women." Keep in mind that 2007 was before the economic crash and the resulting Great Recession, which has exacerbated the situation of the middle class.

The continuing decline of the middle class is most solidly stated in a 2013 book by French economist Thomas Piketty, called ***Capital in the Twenty-First Century***. The book reveals that the rate of capital return in developed countries is greater than the rate of economic growth, and that this imbalance will cause wealth inequality to increase in the future. Essentially, what this means is that wealthy people are making money on their investments at a faster and higher rate than everyone else. Hence, they can afford to buy assets, mainly real estate and stocks, and then sell them at prices (to each other) that are out of the range of people with ordinary salaries. A house in a nice suburb, or a center-city apartment, becomes unaffordable for the middle classes.

The overall effect is that prices go up far more quickly than average salaries. Rich people get richer, and everyone else stays the same. In fact, everyone else gets *poorer*, because their salaries don't increase at the same rate as prices do. The eventual economic condition that we are left with is one of feudalism, with two classes: the very rich, and the poor.

Piketty's solution to this problem is for governments to put a tax on "wealth," i.e. a tax on what people have in asset holdings and in the bank. This would mean that if someone has $100 million in assets and savings, he would be taxed on it, even though it wasn't considered income for that year.

As Americans, I think we can assume that we will not see this happen in the U.S. in our lifetime. Our culture would view this as double-taxation, and historically we have always been hostile to taxes. Whatever the case, it won't be happening anytime soon.

Whether or not you feel that the system needs to be changed, you need to earn a living.

Whether or not you feel that the system needs to be changed, you need to earn a living—and a good one, too. You need to ensure that you have a good level of food, clothing, and shelter, and that you are keeping pace with the economy and your peers. Those who want to change the system need to make themselves economically viable first. You can't save others from drowning if you yourself can't swim!

MONEY IS NOT A BAD THING

As mentioned above, there is a temptation in one's teens to dislike the concept of money, to resent it as being destructive to the world, to focus only on its faults. The fact is that money is a necessary evil. Without a standard means of exchange, the world would be even more chaotic. And if the concept of money were abolished tomorrow, it would only be a matter of time before we found another standard means of exchange. Money is a part of life that cannot be dismissed.

You cannot have a financially comfortable life while hating the concept of money, just like you can't have a successful relationship while hating the concept of love. If you don't respect money, it won't respect YOU, and you will not attract money-making opportunities.

If you don't respect money, it won't respect YOU.

Don't wish that things were cheaper. You can't control the prices. Instead, wish that you had more money, and learn how to make that happen.

Money is not meant to be stressed over, to be viewed with such extreme frugality that it loses any enjoyment which it can bring. Money is meant to be spent relatively freely, always within reason, but *freely*, not forcibly. It is not meant to bring you pain. And the less you have of it, the more painful it becomes. Even the *sound* of the word—"money"—becomes painful to your ears when you have none of it. One of the most difficult parts about being poor is having friends who *aren't* poor. You soon realize that they cannot understand your situation, and that you can't keep up with their lifestyle. Ultimately, if you are poor, it affects your friendships.

There is also the daily psychological effect of walking past restaurants and shops, of avoiding making plans with people, just because one can't afford them. Do you want that to be you? Your salary has a strong influence on your lifestyle. Perhaps at this time in your life you are not interested in expensive vacations or nice restaurants; but as you get older, you will be.

While there is a certain dignity in enduring suffering that has been forced on you, there is no pride in being poor. Try being poor for a week and you will have had enough of it to shatter all delusions. People who aspire to be "starving artists" have never experienced what it really means to starve.

You have to ask yourself:

- Do I want to watch my friends, classmates, and peers surpass me?

- Do I want to constantly worry about affording everything?

Human beings are simple in many ways. Most of us want a life of relatively few worries, of achievements, and of comfort and fun. In a country with a shrinking middle class, and less job stability, these are becoming harder to achieve. We need to have an income that allows us to *not* worry about car repair or needing some new clothes, and an income that allows us to go out for a nice dinner and not stress about whether we can afford it.

Finally, going back to the research by Kahneman and Deaton, earning above the salary threshold also has a positive effect on your feeling of life satisfaction. You won't be happy every minute—no one is—but you will have a deeper sense of satisfaction about where your life is going. This is a result of having a financial safety net and a disposable income. Money helps us pursue our hobbies and also to be generous towards others. These things enrich our lives.

2 Direction: Choosing It, and Not Waiting for It

"Direction" refers to the career you want to pursue. Without direction, ability is useless. There are plenty of intelligent, capable people out there who have never reached their full potential because they were unable to focus their career, and because they didn't know which profession to pursue. They sat back and waited for inspiration, which never came. They thought they would fall into their passion, or that their passion would fall into their lap—and it didn't.

Without direction, ability is useless.

It may come as a surprise that college does not give you direction. College teaches you what you choose (i.e. what you pay) to be taught. College assumes that you have already found your direction—that is, your career—and fills the role of teaching you the courses you have selected. Hence, college is a tool, not a guide. It does not give you guidance on what to be.

Nor, unfortunately, does high school. Guidance Counselors in high schools are occupied with their relationships with colleges: writing recommendation letters, providing documentation that is requested, maintaining contacts, and so forth. High schools' main emphasis is on getting students into college, as this is a measurable way of showing their school's effectiveness.

Both high schools and colleges work with the assumption that you know what career direction you want to take. They don't invest time in giving you career advice, even though it is essential to the rest of your life. And hence it remains up to you to find this direction, and to find it before you go to college, so you can choose the right major and courses.

Some people are lucky to know their career direction when they are very young. My cousin went to the doctor's office when she was five years old and walked out saying, "Mommy, I want to be a doctor when I grow up." And she is. Engineers tend to know from their early teens that an engineering job appeals to them. Nevertheless, for most of us, finding the right career depends on doing our own research, not flashes of inspiration. High school and college aren't going to do that research for you.

As the author Jack London once said, "You cannot wait for inspiration. You have to go after it with a club." I have met many people in their late 20s, and indeed well into their 30s, who are still waiting for that moment where their direction is revealed to them. At those ages, they are already so far behind that it has harmed their sense of confidence. Equally badly, they will be starting from the bottom in the career that they choose, with a low salary and a younger boss. Age is a significant factor in a boss or manager, and most bosses in their 20s lack the maturity and experience to manage people, regardless of how many degrees those bosses may have.

Factors in Direction

Choosing your direction is not all about how you feel inside—it also depends on a number of external factors.

Fundamentally, choosing your direction involves thinking about what you can do, what you like to do, and what will pay you enough to have a financially comfortable life. We are taught to not admit our limitations, but we should not deny that they exist, lest we delude ourselves. If you like chemistry, but have had trouble passing even the most basic high school chemistry tests (despite giving 100% effort), it is likely that chemistry is not the direction for you. As the world of athletics illustrates, passion and hard work are not always enough to make you a success. Innate ability, unfortunately, is also a critical factor.

A good friend of mine who loved mathematics encountered a similar situation. Despite his passion, it took him four times as long to do his high school math homework as other students, and he foresaw himself falling behind if he majored in math and sat in high-level classes with all the math "whizzes". But his fondness for numbers encouraged him to major in Finance, where he excelled (financial math is easier than theoretical math, as I will explain later). Now, he has a very well-paying job and still pursues his love of math as a hobby. What did he do? He took his passion and used it in an area where he was more effective. And he is a lot happier for it.

Similarly, you can be fond of a certain career, and have the skills, but you must also pay attention to whether it pays you a decent wage. "Loving what you do" does not, in itself, pay the bills, and a job is not a "good" job unless it provides financial comfort.

A job is not a "good" job unless it provides financial comfort.

"Follow Your Dreams"

Most of us have been hearing "follow your dreams" since we were in kindergarten. The fault in this statement is that not everyone has lofty fantasies about their professional future. Most people are happy to just have a financially comfortable life. At the age of 17, after four years of grueling high school, with nonstop tests and exams and papers, you may not exactly be full of dreams. For the past four years, and indeed for your whole career as a student, school has given you your goals. Now, suddenly, you are asked to come up with them out of the blue.

All this pressure to have dreams can be misleading. You don't need to have dreams to have a happy and financially comfortable life. You do, however, need to have a *plan.* Instead of waiting around for dreams and inspiration, which may never come, you need to look at what is practical in enabling you to have a life of relative comfort.

THE FORMULA FOR DIRECTION

Start with the salary that you want. It has to at least match our threshold of $88,000 per year, as there's no point pursuing a career if it won't pay you a liveable wage. After that, find out which jobs and careers will pay you that amount. Once you have that list, you can decide which careers on it you like and which careers you are capable of doing. This decision process just requires research, which is easily done over the internet. During this research, you find out what is required to get into that career: which major and which qualifications. Essentially, you are starting with the salary that you want and then working backwards to see how to get it.

It's that simple.

SUCCESS IN SCHOOL VS. SUCCESS IN LIFE

It is often said that "success in school does not translate into success in life." This is largely due to the lack of direction that schools provide. But it is also true in itself: many professions lack the predictability and structure that school offers. In school, you know exactly what you need to do to get an "A". High school and college both give you constant goals to reach. But life does not give you these clear goals; you have to define them for yourself, which is difficult. The advice in this book will define those goals for you.

A career in medicine offers one of the closest relationships between scholastic and professional success: the harder you work—i.e. the more you learn—the greater the chance that you can do your work effectively. You can read book after book, do lab after lab, and you'll have seen the vast proportion of cases that will come before you in the field. There is a stability found in knowledge.

Business, especially if you want to own your own firm, is the opposite. The sheer task of making someone part with his money, especially for non-essential reasons, is one of the hardest on Earth, and is constantly changing. The more you involve people's wishes and tastes, the less predictable your job is, and hence the weaker the relationship between your success in school and success in life. Note, however, that many business jobs, such as accounting, have a good degree of stability. The more you deal directly with customers, the less predictability you have.

Life isn't one big harvest—you need to spend time planting the seeds.

The most important aspect of direction is understanding that you must *have* a direction. Having a plan is better than having no plan. Life isn't one big harvest—you need to spend time planting the seeds, and you need to know how to plant the right seeds, and in the right way. It can be tough, but a little pain now is better than a lot of regret later.

In the following sections, I will be giving you the resources to have direction, while talking about specific majors and jobs. Do not trust inspiration or fate to find direction for you.

3 Majors: The Ones That Get You Hired

Your path to success starts before you step on a college campus. It starts with your choice of major. Choosing a major is one of the most important decisions you'll ever make.

Choosing a major is one of the most important decisions you'll ever make.

We all go to college with the goal of improving our lives. Yet for many people, that's about as specific as their plan gets. Confronted with having to make a choice, they choose a major based on whether they think it will be fun, and often it is not a practical one. Hence, when they graduate, they realize that they are no more employable than they were four years before. Such individuals are then paralyzed in their pursuit to be successful, by having made a bad choice of major. They spend the rest of their lives playing catch-up, unable to proactively take charge of their professional lives, but always depending on opportunities to come to them rather than dictating what opportunities they will have.

As stated earlier, success in school does not mean financial comfort in life. Financial comfort depends more upon the direction that you take. People who are average students in high school can pursue Finance degrees and take jobs in financial management, and earn far more than fellow alumni who pursued non-lucrative careers. So direction is just as important as one's ability, and arguably more so.

Choosing the wrong major means that instead of using the rest of your life to capitalize on a good decision, you'll be spending it trying to make the best of a *bad* decision. There is a world of difference.

The College Industry

The notion of the "need" to go to college is one of the most successful business ideas of the 20th century. College wasn't always a necessity for a career. The concept of a university originated as a means of training young men for careers in the Church. In the 1600s, with the Scientific Revolution, it also became a place for education in the sciences. Meanwhile it was also a place for wealthy young men to complete a classical education (Latin and Greek) and to socialize with *other* wealthy young men. College, for many, was not seen as a springboard for a career; rather, it was a form of recreation, and many students left without bothering to complete their studies.

However, in the past seven decades the college industry has succeeded in turning the concept of going to college into a necessity. A college degree is now needed for most jobs, and there is no substitute. Colleges have made themselves an oligopoly, and can raise their prices at high rates each year without any fear of losing customers.

All colleges are businesses, in the same way that automobile firms, computer companies, convenience stores, and banks are businesses: they need customers in order to make money, and they want to maximize what customers pay them. Colleges sell education, rather than cars or laptops, but colleges are businesses all the same.

As such, a college's main interest in you is your money. Therefore, you must treat a college as you would treat any other business you deal with. You want to get as much out of them as you can. You want to make the most out of the money you are spending on them.

Treat a college as you would treat any other business you deal with.

The reason that colleges offer majors that don't lead to jobs is because there are still plenty of people out there who will pay for them. These people haven't been given proper guidance, and are still choosing majors which will leave them unemployed. Like a good business, a college's main concern is to make money. If enough people wanted to study Gum Chewing, colleges would invent a major for it, regardless of the major's uselessness.

During my senior year of high school, I received a letter from a college in Florida, which trumpeted their Philosophy program. Composed in very motivating language, it was probably written by a professional marketing agency—I am sure that most colleges hire one. The letter celebrated how many of the college's teachers had PhDs, the awards they had won and books they had written, the interesting courses they offered, and how enriched I would be. It made me feel that I'd be on top of the world as a Philosophy major if I went there. Aside from saying "Buy Now," it had all the ingredients of an advertisement.

Don't be deceived by the well-crafted promotional language used by colleges. Look at them with scrutiny, and use them in the way that you, as a customer, would use any other service-provider. As a customer, you should view their function as that of preparing you for the working world. Make sure they live up to their end of the bargain.

How to Choose Your Major—the Majors That Lead to Jobs

I find it impossible to talk about majors without talking about careers. Unfortunately, colleges are perfectly happy to talk about majors as though they were an end in themselves. Colleges are mentally stuck in the 1950s, when having a college degree in anything was sufficient to guarantee employment. But times have changed.

To begin, I'm amazed when people say that they don't want to study business because it won't teach them enough about the world. If money isn't a huge dimension of the world, and of life, what is? Learning about money helps you to learn about the world. Money is an essential aspect of everyone's lives.

Most well-paid professions are heavy on the "front end," requiring degrees and qualifications to be earned. Yes, this takes time, hard work, and living like a pauper for a few years. There are no shortcuts. Nonetheless, always keep in mind that a little pain now is better than a lot of regret later. It's easier to be poor at 23 than at 43, both socially and psychologically.

It's easier to be poor at 23 than at 43.

Numbers vs. Letters

The old saying, "There's safety in numbers," applies to armies as well as the type of job you choose.

Let's look at the majors that lead straight to professions:

- Finance
- Engineering
- Computer Science

- Information Technology
- Accounting
- Chemistry and other sciences

Do you notice something about these majors? They all involve *numbers*. When you are good with numbers, you can prove your worth to a company and an employer. And as I illustrate below, anyone can be good with numbers.

A major that focuses on numbers enables a future employer to quantify your worth.

A major that focuses on numbers enables a future employer to quantify your worth. Majoring in a "Letters" major does not enable this, and hence your value is constantly being called into question. The more quantifiable you are, the more employable you are. Careers that involve numbers rather than letters—that is, analyzing numerical information rather than writing—have more employability, more stability, and pay more money. In an October 2016 survey by Glassdoor of the *50 Highest-Paying College Majors*, the top 15 were all engineering, computer science/IT, and finance/ accounting, with nursing as the only exception.

There is a misconception that numbers-based jobs require extensive skills in higher math. This is entirely false. You don't need to be a whiz in math, or even to have taken the higher-level courses. As an

Accounting professor said to me once (a man who also made a fortune as a private consultant), "I can add, subtract, multiply, and divide—that's all I can do". In other words, if you have passed pre-Algebra, you can do any job requiring numbers. Complicated mathematical procedures have been put into formulas which computers can do for you.

There is a beauty in numbers—the beauty of objectivity. Numbers provide a clarity, an unambiguity, that words do not. Someone who is "good with numbers" will always be valued by a company. A company's viability is proven by its figures, not by its words. And as long as you can do basic math, you can be good with numbers.

Having a "minor" in one of these numbers subjects is not enough. Companies care about your *major*, and will ignore whatever you have minored in. Don't sucker yourself into choosing a "fun" major and a practical minor.

Even for aspiring lawyers, it is recommended to study a numbers-based major. People will say, "You should study a major that has a lot of writing," but all majors these days involve plenty of writing. Furthermore, studying business or engineering will prepare you for many fields of Law. You can always take a minor in a more writing-based subject to improve your writing skills.

One problem with letters-based jobs is that they are so subjective. People have widely different views on what constitutes a "good" writer, nor are there formal qualifications for what makes a writer "good." On the other hand, when you tell an employer that you are an accountant with a CPA degree, they know what you can do, and what you are capable of. Remember: employers will look for every excuse NOT to hire you.

Employers will look for every excuse NOT to hire you.

"Should I major in Finance or Economics?"

I am often asked by prospective college students whether they should choose to major in Finance or Economics. In the eyes of an employer, Finance means that you know how to make investments, understand cash flow, and balance the books. Economics means that you have learned a lot of theories—theories which, incidentally, haven't even helped "expert" economists predict economic recessions or depressions. Economists are regarded as having the same reliability as weathermen. In short, Finance is a practical major, while Economics is not.

MAJORS THAT DON'T LEAD TO JOBS

Just because you are told to follow your passion does not mean that you need to follow it in a professional context. If your passion is European Folklore, you have to accept that there are very few opportunities out there where you can derive an income from specializing in this field. The same goes for Ancient History and quite a few others.

If you have a passion similar to these, follow it in your free time. There are tons of websites, clubs, blogs, etc., in which you can pursue these passions, and with the advent of self-publishing, you can still write your own book on the subject and contribute to the field.

You certainly don't need to major in these areas, nor should you, as they don't lead to employment. Consider yourself lucky that you have an intellectual passion to pursue in your free time, rather than just waiting for the next sports season to start or for the next TV series. It's better to be an accountant who has an extracurricular hobby in European Folklore, than a European Folklore expert who is unemployed.

One of my friends refers to such majors as folklore, philosophy, and art history as "hobby majors." Although they are textbook-based, these majors are not much different in nature from any other hobby, like skiing or scuba-diving. Like a hobby, such majors are fun and interesting. But it's not worth it to pursue them as a *major*, with the time and expense that could be used for something practical.

I am not saying that courses such as Anthropology, Philosophy, and History are not important. They *are* important, and valuable in many ways. Unfortunately, employers are keen to hire people who understand balance sheets and investments, not those who have studied Picasso and the Trojan War. If you have a passion for these subjects, you can of course buy the books and study them yourself, or even minor in them. Furthermore, you can "audit" them. To audit a course means to take the course but not write papers or take exams, and to hence not receive a grade. But please don't pay *40,000 dollars a year* for them. Do them on your own time, not on your money's time. The most important thing is to have a major that leads to a job.

Employers are keen to hire people who understand balance sheets and investments.

Hobby majors are for children of wealthy families, kids who are going to inherit wealth or daddy's company, who are not dependent on college education to get a job or to have a comfortable income. These majors are *not* for middle-class students who will need a job and a career that provide financial comfort. People who major in these subjects often end up scrounging for low-paying jobs in media or marketing—often jobs with low stability, which are completely dependent on the state of the economy. When the economy gets tough, their jobs are the first to be cut.

For a list of the majors with the most unemployed graduates, a survey from April 2017 can be found at www.startclass.com.

Be cautious also about studying languages as a major. I am surprised at the number of people who go to college and study Spanish. A company that is in need of a Spanish-speaker will most likely hire someone who has grown up in the U.S. speaking both Spanish and English. If you really want to study a language, study it as a minor.

Ask yourself: Do I want to wake up every morning and wish I had studied something else, and realize that it is too late? Do I want to be a college graduate who is hoping and praying just to get *any* job? Do I want to feel directionless, unstable, and constantly unsure of whether I'd be able to find another job if I got laid off?

Those who are adamant about pursuing hobby majors often use the same platitudes in their defense:

"WELL, I COULD ALWAYS BECOME A LAWYER."

Law School is a commitment of three tough years of study, $200,000, and then the grueling early years at a law firm. Furthermore, the type of person who enjoys contemplative acts such as reading romantic poetry or studying 19th century art is very different from the person who works in a confrontational profession like Law. In short, you should only go into law if you want to be a lawyer, not because it is a last resort.

"I COULD ALWAYS JUST GO INTO SALES."

I did sales for six years. Sales is the only job I know which never gets easier, no matter how long you do it.

Why? Because no matter how good a salesman you are, you are always up against the fact that the customer has the complete and absolute freedom to say "No." You cannot force him, regardless of how persuasive you may be. With the fact that sales positions are largely paid on commissions, it means that you essentially are never sure where your next paycheck is coming from, or how much it will be. Salespeople have trouble planning family trips because they don't know if they will be earning enough when it comes time for the vacation.

These days, Sales—or "Business Development," as it is often euphemistically called—is actually harder than ever, as customers are more informed. The salesman is no longer the primary source of information, and customers can check and compare prices online. According to the Social Media Authority website, www.socialmedia-authority.com, 77% of buyers insist on doing their own independent research before even talking to a salesperson. And this figure is increasing every year.

In sales, you are only as good as your last sale. A bad week or month is enough to have your boss breathing down your neck and the threat of termination. But a job that requires certificates is different, because you always have the certificates to back you up. While of course you will bring your best every day, you don't have to *prove* every day that you are qualified. The certificate does it for you.

"I CAN ALWAYS BE AN AUTHOR OR A JOURNALIST."

As someone who has worked in the publishing sphere, I can tell you an industry secret: the average book sells between 50 and 150 copies over the author's lifetime. The qualification for being a "best-seller" is sales of 5,000 copies. You won't be getting fat royalty checks off sales of 5,000 books, and certainly not off 150. Most of the authors who make millions of dollars are the ones you already know: Stephen King, James Patterson, J.K. Rowling, John Grisham, and a handful of others. The remaining hundreds of thousands of authors do not make a living from their writing.

As for journalism, the career of Journalist has been gradually eroded over the last 30 years by the practices of wealthy press barons and by the Internet. It is no longer a profession which yields a middle-class income. While working in the business media field, e.g. writing for the ***Financial Times***, can yield a liveable wage, it requires interacting with arrogant CEOs and stockbrokers—who will earn at least ten times what you earn—while needing to know as much about the market as they do. If you are going to learn that much about finance, you might as well just *do* finance, rather than write about it.

THE "BEING WELL-ROUNDED" FALLACY

Jacks-of-all-trades are out of style. It is fashionable to say that employers are looking to

Jacks-of-all-trades are out of style.

hire people who are "well-rounded," and some *employers* may even claim to want well-rounded staff, but the fact is that they want people who are very capable at a particular skill. Employers are looking for people that they can hire with a minimum (or no) training, and who are completely focused on their industry and that particular position being offered.

The era of apprenticeships is unfortunately over. Companies want you to hit the ground running. While employers do provide "training," it is training on how to use their particular software or sell their particular product—not on how to do the job itself. Again, people do not get hired for being well-rounded. They get hired for having specific knowledge in a specific area. You need to focus your attention on an area that will make you gainfully employed. No company advertises for a jack-of-all-trades.

No company advertises for a jack-of-all-trades.

"But CEOs are well-rounded!" Yes, CEOs are well-rounded because they have usually had at least 25 years of work experience.

Do not be deceived by people who say companies want well-rounded individuals. We hear, "Employers want people who know how to *think*!" There's plenty of thinking that goes on in finance, accounting, engineering, and IT. This thinking has a practical bent, though you'll be surprised at how much creativity and thinking on your feet can be required.

Finally, I'll offer one corollary to choosing majors based on passions. This is for the person who is so intense about pursuing a certain career that he is willing to die for it. There are those who aspire to be filmmakers or artists or musicians, etc., who simply cannot imagine not pursuing their dream. How do you know if you are one of these people? Here's how: if this passion causes you to forget to eat and shower, to break plans with friends, to wake up and fall asleep thinking about it, and is the ruling thought in your mind each and every day over the course of at least two years, then you qualify. Most people who put their "passions" through this test realize that their passion is really just a hobby.

PROACTIVELY FINDING DIRECTION

How do we define "work"? There are different ways, but one definition that I use is, "Things you need to do in order to be financially comfortable." Some may call it cynical, but there's no getting around the fact that work itself is something we need to do, not necessarily something we want.

Again, it boils down to direction. You must *choose* your career direction. It will not come to you in a flash of inspiration. Whether you choose now or wait until your 30s, in both cases you will still be the one who chooses.

But if you wait, you lose valuable time, and watch your friends and peers surpass you. A lack of professional direction is a life-threatening disease—psychologically, financially, and after a short while, physically.

A lack of professional direction is a life-threatening disease.

Do not go to college with a "blank slate" as to what you want to do. You need to start carving out a path early. Yes, in life you'll find the occasional person who didn't know what he wanted to do and became successful. But you'll find a lot more who didn't.

As self-help guru Jim Rohn says, "If you don't design your own life plan, chances are you'll fall into someone else's plan. And guess what they have planned for you? Not much."

In addition to the "being well-rounded" fallacy, beware of these kinds of advice:

- **The "first job" myth:** I was told that a first job was just a "first job"—that is, you took it just to enter the workforce, and it was merely a starting point. But imagine if that weren't the case: imagine that if, six months before you graduated, you knew that you had a good job waiting for you. And you had the confidence in knowing that that job had levels through which you could ascend and measure your progress. You had a tangible beginning to your work life. A first job should not just be a first job, and to think like this is to put less pressure on yourself to start off on the right track. A first job should be the beginning of a positive, successful work career.

- **People telling you that a particular job is "boring":** The careers that pay you an income that meets our $88,000 threshold are indeed serious, but that does not mean that they are boring. *At all.* Deciding where the company should spend millions (or billions) of dollars, traveling to a new country to open an office, and other aspects of the "numbers" professions are certainly not boring. Bear in mind that once you get caught up in the momentum of nearly any job, you have way too much going on to feel bored. There will be constant activity, and decisions that affect a lot of people.

- **"Don't work for someone else—just be your own boss":** Yes, it's great to have tons of ideas, and the thought of becoming an entrepreneur is attractive to many. However, being an entrepreneur is not for everyone. It is a seven-day-a-week job, and you do most of the administrative and managerial work yourself, including accounting and HR. One aspect that many people don't think about when they consider being an entrepreneur is cash flow. A huge problem that entrepreneurs face is getting clients to pay their bills, and especially getting them to pay the bills on time. Without the bills being paid, you can't pay your overheads, particularly your staff!

- **"It's *who* you know, not *what* you know":** Connections are great—if you are focused, if you have direction. If you don't, they can actually make things worse, as they cause your attention to be scattered. You start to depend on having connections in order to give you focus—which having connections will not do. Beware of thinking that a large network is an asset in itself. A network is only useful if you already know what career you want. Many young people spend a lot of time at meetings and dinners that lead them nowhere or get them off-track and involved in fruitless endeavours—all because of a faith that "having connections" will bring them success. It leads them farther and farther away from a focused perspective. Connections come in handy when you are already qualified, not on their own.

  A network is only useful if you already know what career you want.

- **"Robots will do your job in a few years":** Stay away from negative people who are always saying "the sky is falling" and "such-and-such profession

> is going to be obsolete in a few years." Robert Kiyosaki, in his book ***Rich Dad, Poor Dad***, calls this the "Chicken Little" scenario. When I was in college over 20 years ago, I heard this scaremongering with regard to various professions, and all of them are still going strong. Ironically, journalism, which was one of the careers cited as being a job for life, now fails to provide a liveable income. So don't pay attention to these ominous forecasts of the future.

Lastly, don't listen to such advice as "If you can't be the best at something, don't do it." There will always be someone out there who is better, because people are always striving to improve themselves. The best accountant today is not necessarily the best accountant tomorrow. Imagine if everyone only pursued a career if they thought they would be the best? It is indeed noble to push yourself to the limit, but don't be put off by the idea that you may not be at the top of the top. And so, to end with a little joke: What do they call the guy who graduates last in his medical class? "Doctor"!

4 Careers: Living Comfortably

The transition from a major to a career should be as seamless as possible.

The transition from a major to a career should be as seamless as possible. That is, your major should be a preface to your career, and your career should follow directly from your major. Hence, there is no "limbo" period of graduating from college and not knowing what you want to do.

Any career should be one that pays you a liveable wage and allows you to grow within the career. Growth is vertical, hence the metaphor, of "climbing the ladder."

But let's go into more specific terms. We often hear about someone who has a "good" job. What does this actually mean?

Defining a "Good" Job

Aside from salary, the definition of a good job begins with this simple principle: A "good" job is a job that you *like* on the good days and can *tolerate* on the bad days. There is no such thing as a job you *love* doing every day. And this is simply because work is called "work" for a reason. If it was always fun and easy, you wouldn't be paid to do it.

The idea of the "perfect" job is a myth. First of all, there is no such thing as a "perfect" job. The phrase is a contradiction in terms. Don't bother searching for the perfect job or career. It doesn't exist. Every job has something about it that is annoying. Doctors have to give bad news to patients—sometimes news that is tragic. In finance, you can lose the company's money. College professors have to spend whole weekends at the end of the semester grading essays and exams. Accountants work long hours during tax season. The list goes on and on, and the right approach is to not mistake the part for the whole. Don't judge a profession based on one conversation. Keep things in perspective, and remember that every job has its bad days. Perfectionism has no place in real life or real jobs.

Another myth is that a good job is one that is easy. Quite simply, easy jobs are not good jobs. They get boring fast, they don't teach you new things, and they don't keep you growing. Growth is necessary if you want to stay employable and financially viable. The best people in any industry are those who are learning more than their counterparts. While it is less stressful to be complacent,

The best people in any industry are those who are learning more than their counterparts.

ultimately complacency is self-destructive. Fortunately or unfortunately, you need to keep climbing—you can't stay static for too long.

Still another characteristic of a good job is your salary. Don't be fooled by those who say "Salary is not important—do what you love." Money, as we have discussed, is important as a foundation for your happiness. True, it cannot buy happiness directly, but it enables you to have the freedom to focus on things besides your basic needs. When people tell you that "money doesn't matter as long as you love what you do," they are trivializing the condition of being poor. People who say that "money doesn't matter" have never been in a state of having no money.

If your salary is lower than the threshold we have discussed, you will have to accept that the financial part of your life will be difficult—which means nearly every part of your life will be difficult. It's easy to talk about being poor for 50 or 60 years when you are 17, as you probably have never spent a day worried about where your next meal is coming from. Don't forget that each of those 50 years contains 365 days, all of which have 24 hours. Try being poor, unsure of your food, accommodation, or clothing situation, or of your employment, for a week, and imagine that being your status for the rest of your life. No: salary is tremendously important. Regarding job security, these days your security comes from your knowledge and ability, not from your company. The more qualifications you have, the more stability you will have.

SCALABILITY

Ideally, one wants to choose an industry that is "scalable," meaning that your product or service has the capability to be enlarged without dramatically increasing your workload, idea, or process (in short, your costs).

Computer software is an example of scalability. Once the software is developed, it can then be sold online to millions of people, without an increase in personnel, or being changed for each customer. Scalability is also seen in finance and asset management, with regard to the way stocks and land appreciate over time.

Areas where we don't see scalability are jobs where a human being is needed and time is inflexible. For the most part, teachers' jobs are not scalable, and neither are writers'. The latter are paid by assignment, and assignments need to be written from scratch each time. However, if a teacher were to record her lectures and then sell them over the internet, she would be making her job scalable. Writers such as Stephen King, who spend three months writing a novel and then sell it to millions, have made their profession scalable. But scalability is much harder to achieve in these fields.

A career does not necessarily have to be scalable to earn you a good salary. Doctors do not have a particularly scalable job. They can only treat one patient at a time. However, the reason why doctors' fees are high is because when you see a doctor, you are not just paying for her time; you are also paying for all the years of study and experience she has done to gain the required knowledge. The careers that are heavy on the front-end, i.e. with more degrees and certificates required, enable you to make more money.

What Constitutes a Good Company?

A good company is one which:

- Pays you on time, and with a liveable income
- Has an environment that allows for upward communication with superiors
- Provides a clean working environment
- Keeps up with technology
- Provides training so you can improve yourself (many companies are reluctant to do this, as it means people will leave after the training, for better jobs)
- Understands the need for you to have a private life, i.e. has a work-life balance
- Has power distributed between several executives, not run like a dictatorship

- Does not expect you to eat your lunch at your desk
- Has a system of "recourse," where you can speak to other superiors besides your immediate supervisor

A Good Boss

While we're at it, here is some information on what constitutes a good boss. Just like a bad teacher or professor can ruin a course, so can a bad boss ruin your job (though not your career). The main qualities for a good boss are:

- Self-control
- An even temper
- A concept of work-life balance
- Receptiveness to ideas
- An interest in seeing you grow—which means taking time to mentor or at least instruct you

The top two points rule out most people under 30. Management skills are learned over time, with experience, and cannot simply be taught in a classroom.

Working Corporate vs. Working for an Entrepreneur

Due to the massive success of entrepreneurs in the IT industry, the concept of working in a start-up firm is very hot at the moment. But what is it like working for these people?

Working for an entrepreneur is similar to being the advisor to a king, especially in a small company. The king has all the power. You are dependent on his moods and have to adjust accordingly. There is no recourse if he is being unfair to you. The corporate world is better on this point, in that it provides a system of recourse, whether found in the HR department or another senior manager.

Another large difference is seen in idea generation. In a small company, such as that owned by an entrepreneur, your ideas can reach fruition fast, and by only needing one approval—from the owner. In corporate, ideas have to go through a bureaucratic process, where many people contribute and perhaps change the idea, before the final decision is made. In short, in the corporate world it takes longer to put new ideas into action.

Researching Careers

We live in the Golden Age for researching careers. As recently as the 1990s, the process of researching careers boiled down to who you could ask. After your family, you got as far as your friend's parents. Now, by typing a few words into Google, you can get pages upon pages of information on "a day in the life of" any field you specify. While there are specific websites such as www.careercornerstone.org, your best bet is to check out as many links as possible from your search. There will be YouTube videos as well. There is no excuse for not thoroughly researching a career.

There is no excuse for not thoroughly researching a career.

To get you started on your career research, I have done a little homework for you. Below are descriptions for professions in accounting, finance, and IT. All of these have salaries within our desired range, and quite above it, in nearly all cases:

ACCOUNTING POSITIONS

Jobs for accountants are expected to grow at the steady rate of 13% through 2022, according to the U.S. Bureau of Labor Statistics.

Corporate controller: most businesses have a company controller who tracks and handles various financial aspects of the company. Controllers set financial goals for the firm, prepare the firm's taxes, supervise the other finance and accounting employees, and control how the budget will be managed—and spent.

Finance director: this is the individual who supervises all finance managers and functions, including budget, credit, insurance, tax, treasury, and accounting. The finance director is often the top finance job for small firms. For larger firms, the finance director is second to the CFO.

CFO: the Chief Financial Officer is the top financial position in a large firm. The CFO has to have a more "macro" vision than the finance director, while also being able to manage risk and be responsible for the firm's financial planning. A CFO reports directly to upper management, and is often on the Board of Directors.

Cost accounting manager: handles the implementation of cost accounting methods and activities. A cost accounting manager is responsible for (not surprisingly) "costing", managing cost audits, and compliance, while also preparing internal cost reports.

Budget analyst: focuses on the guidelines for the firm's annual budget, as well as how funds are distributed throughout the company.

Auditor: auditors generally work for an accounting firm and service external clients. They examine a firm's financial statements, making sure that all information is correct—and legal.

Treasury analyst: works with the accounting, finance, and any other finance-related departments. Treasury analysts look at assets and liabilities, credit, cash flow, and any other financial activity.

FINANCE POSITIONS

Aside from earning good money, one of the benefits of a finance job is that you learn what to *do* with money: how to manage it, and how to dominate it rather than fear it.

Forecasts for finance-related jobs are also extremely positive, according to the Bureau of Labor Statistics. For example, employment of financial analysts is projected to grow 12% from 2014 to 2024, faster than the average for all occupations. A growing range of financial products and the need for in-depth knowledge of geographic regions are expected to lead to strong employment growth.

Actuary: the job of actuary is consistently rated one of the best careers in the U.S., for income, work-life balance, and stress levels, as well as job openings. An actuary measures and manages risk for insurance companies as well as for a multiplicity of industries, such as banking, investment management, the government, pension programs, and consulting. A number of examinations are required to become an actuary, and hence it is heavy on the front-end, though most of these exams can be taken while you are already employed. As said, a little pain in your early 20s is better than a lot of regret later on.

> ***The job of actuary is consistently rated one of the best careers in the U.S., for income, work-life balance, and stress levels, as well as job openings.***

Money manager: money managers are on the "buy" side of Wall Street, meaning that they make stock recommendations to their company, usually by sector. The qualification of Chartered Financial Analyst (CFA) is required. They are skilled quantitatively, and often have more specific titles of Portfolio Manager or Research Analyst.

CFO: see above.

Corporate finance: this position involves financially running and growing the business. Often, it involves giving input on mergers and acquisitions.

Financial analyst: mentioned above, a financial analyst looks at a firm's investments, expenses, risk, and overall financial history. They then make recommendations for investments, in alignment with the goals put down by the firm.

Insurance underwriter: evaluates the level of risk that you pose when you are a customer of an insurance firm, and determines your premium and extent of coverage. Underwriters have to find the right balance between being conservative (i.e. less attractive to customers because of the high premiums) and liberal (which may result in too many insurance claims by customers).

Real estate/Asset management: we commonly think of real estate as selling houses, often something done on a part-time basis. However, the world of commercial and industrial property, as well as real estate investment, is rich with the potential for solid, well-paying jobs—for which a finance degree is a method of entry. This would include real estate brokerages (firms like CBRE and Jones Lang Lasalle), real estate developers (Tishman Speyer), and real estate investment (Blackstone). Asset management refers to making sure properties are profitable, as well as buying and then selling them for a profit. Other finance-informed property positions include real estate valuation, as well as jobs in the highly lucrative construction industry, such as quantity surveyor.

Wealth manager/Financial planner: this career involves advising individuals and families on how to save and invest their money. A financial planner will be familiar with stocks, bonds, and mutual funds, among other investment methods. The CFA qualification is a great help. The term "wealth manager" is a synonym, usually used by financial planners who have clients classified as High Net Worth Individuals.

COMPUTER SCIENCE AND IT POSITIONS

Not surprisingly, the Bureau of Labor Statistics also has very auspicious forecasts for computer science and IT. Employment of computer and information technology occupations is projected to grow 12% from 2014 to 2024.

IT consultant: what is interesting about an IT consultant is that you are a kind of "doctor." Just as a doctor knows about the body, you know about the computer—and when people need you, they need you urgently and are willing to pay what is required. IT consultants understand operating systems and how to make computers run faster and more reliably. Every company needs IT consultants, whether the firm is small or large.

Cloud architect: oversees a company's cloud computing strategy. This involves designing apps, cloud adoption plans, and various other cloud-related responsibilities.

Web developer: websites are of critical importance for any company these days, and hence this position is very valuable. Web developers create a firm's website, with pages, apps, and content. They need to have a sense of design and what will make a site work efficiently and in a user-friendly way. A web developer will also know some of the web languages, especially Javascript and HTML.

Software engineer: is involved in the design, development, implementation, testing, and maintenance of software. They are also called software developers. As some of these positions are being outsourced, it will be important to have coding skills as well as interpersonal skills, such that you can communicate well with upper management—who will most likely not be familiar with technical jargon.

IT vendor manager: oversees a firm's supply of IT, both hardware and software. In this position, you would build relationships with suppliers and evaluate their quality, prices, and delivery efficiency.

Data modeler: this position is becoming more complicated, and more necessary, as we rely more and more on computers. Data modeling involves creating a structure for data, which is used in information systems, to achieve overall seamlessness and compatibility.

Mobile application developer: this is a hugely important position, with so many businesses making themselves available on cell phones. The rate at which consumers do research and make purchases on their phones is rising dramatically each year, and hence the ability to create apps that facilitate business is critical.

ENGINEERING POSITIONS

For engineering, there are of course a number of fields one can enter, and some of it just depends on your personal preference. Civil, mechanical, and industrial engineers continue to earn salaries that surpass our salary threshold of $88,000, as do electrical, biomedical, and chemical engineers. Marine and materials engineers also earn competitive incomes. In fact, it is difficult to find an area of engineering that does not pay well. Employment

It is difficult to find an area of engineering that does not pay well.

of biomedical engineers is projected to grow 23% from 2014 to 2024, while that of civil engineers is expected to grow at a slower but still healthy rate of 8% during that period.

"Appealing" Jobs

"What if none of these lucrative careers appeal to me?" Then you need to re-examine how you are judging what is "appealing." Don't make it mandatory that your work has to match your intellectual interests. Most of the "fun" jobs don't pay you enough to live comfortably. With the money you earn from a "good" job—which we have defined as one that you will like on the good days and tolerate on the bad—you can pursue your passions on weeknights, weekends, and vacations. If your passion is indeed history or anthropology or philosophy, you can even read on your lunch break, as I do.

When you think of what makes a job "appealing," think of career development, employability, salary, and stability. Focus on the things that help you live. Don't condemn yourself to a life of "fun" jobs and just scraping by—a life of wondering where your next job will come from, of being scared to death of being laid off.

You will find that when you reach 30, you are socially expected to be on a path to a successful career. I've known some people who were rich by the time they were 30. They all say that there was a bit of luck involved—generally, being in the right place or industry at the right time. All of them worked hard. But what else contributed to their success?

- Being *prepared* for luck: we often hear that luck is a result of hard work, but it's not—luck is not a "result" of anything. (That's why it's called "luck"!) However, luck does favor those who are prepared. And the hard work is the preparation for when that lucky opportunity finally presents itself. We can prepare by making sure we are healthy in both mind and body, that we have a positive perspective, and that we have amassed the right degrees and qualifications.

- Working with direction, and being organized and punctual. There are many books about goals, but I will say that for the 17- to 19-year-old, your goal is to settle on a career path that will allow you a financially comfortable life.

- Starting off properly, with the right major. You can start your career off on the right foot before you even set foot on a college campus, just by choosing a major that leads to gainful employment.

- Staying in the same industry. DO NOT DABBLE. People will tell you that "It's Never Too Late" to start something new, but this doesn't apply to a career. At a certain point, it *is* too late. For some professions, "too late" can be in your 30s, and for some it is even in one's 20s. Don't be fooled by idle phrases tossed out by idealists. Get started on the right path and do not spend valuable years bouncing around from career to career and job to job. If you absolutely must explore, put a stop to it at 25. The people who are happiest when they turn 30 are the ones who have a definite career in front of them and a financial foundation for the future. As the old saying goes, "A rolling stone gathers no moss." In other words, as said above, *do not dabble.*

DO NOT DABBLE.

In some professions, it takes longer to make money: doctors don't start earning well till 35, but after that, their salaries rise more sharply than many other professions.

Alternatives to White-Collar Jobs

Schools and society like to tell us that the white-collar world is the only option. However, the world of the office is not for everyone, and there are indeed alternatives. We have become so seduced by the glamour of being a corporate executive that people often overlook career paths which offer many other advantages.

The Armed Forces

I am always surprised at how many middle-class high school students overlook entering the armed forces. This is usually due to a feeling that the salaries are too low, or to a dislike for the discipline, or because of the feeling that they won't get the full "college experience." What is ignored is that the military offers a ton of benefits: accommodation is free, food is free, healthcare is of course free. Many servicemen end up with more money at the end of the month than those working in corporate middle-management jobs.

Education is also provided: you can pursue a degree while in the military, and much of it is paid for. With college tuition costs rising with no end in sight, and 6% above the rate of inflation (according to research in 2015 by CNBC, in "Why Does a College Degree Cost So Much"), an inexpensive way to get your degree is something to be taken seriously.

The military is also a career in which the requirements for advancement are made clear. It is a reputable and stable career path.

The Trades

Many people go to college but are not academically-minded and can't stand being stuck in a classroom. Quite frankly, they hate school and prefer a hands-on job where they are solving tangible problems, not dealing with office politics. Such individuals are often compelled, by social norms, to attend college and then are forced into a white-collar world which they find uncomfortable. For them, the trades are something to consider.

Let's take being a plumber, for instance. There will always be a need for plumbers—and as you know, when you need a plumber, it is urgent. The job simply requires you to solve problems—no selling, no office politics. It is a skill that customers will always need and will always pay for. You would, of course, go to a vocational college to become an expert in the trade.

While your job stability comes largely from within yourself, there is indeed something to be said for a job where you will always be needed.

"What if I get to my 30s and realize I don't want to be an accountant, engineer, etc.?"

If this does occur, it is still better to have been on a path where you've been earning good money, than to have been on no path. If you have spent ten years in a well-paying career, you'll at least have the money to be able to *afford* making a career change.

Secondly, there is more to making a career change than simply changing your professional focus. By the time you reach your mid-30s, it is likely that you will have a family, a mortgage, or at least a certain lifestyle. These will be important things to consider.

5 Colleges: Where, Why, and How to Choose

I have put my discussion of careers before my discussion of colleges, as you should be thinking of them in that order. There's no point in going to college if you don't have a career that you have chosen to pursue. Students who go to college without a chosen career find themselves jobless after graduation.

There's no point in going to college if you don't have a career that you have chosen to pursue.

Far too much emphasis is put on getting into a "prestigious" college. I'll be quite frank here: unless you go to Harvard or one of its 15–20 counterparts in the pantheon of prestigious institutions, most colleges are perceived as being pretty much the same by employers. The colleges in this special group would comprise the Ivy League schools, a handful of other colleges in New England, and then several colleges in California, the Midwest, and the South. If you go to these schools, it is likely that employers will hire you regardless of your major.

Unfortunately, these schools accept such a small percentage of applicants that one cannot rely on going to them to establish one's future. Acceptance is actually so unpredictable that even high school valedictorians have a low acceptance rate. Each year, these institutions seem to want more and more: high grades, SAT scores, athletics, clubs, etc. In short, one cannot rely on getting into these schools.

The good news is that so few people get into these colleges that you are not likely to be competing with many of them for jobs. Many of these colleges don't offer business or engineering as a major.

I gave myself immense stress in high school about "getting into a good college," as the saying goes, only to later realize that most colleges are "good" and that a college's name alone is not responsible for one's career trajectory.

Here are tips on how to choose a college:

Primary concern

What will be of primary concern, if you go to a college outside of the pantheon mentioned above, is what you choose as your major. I really cannot emphasize this enough. Along with your major, as a priority, are the internship opportunities that a college offers with major firms. Make sure to look into this when you talk with college personnel. The "campus tour" when you visit a college does not provide enough of a perspective to know whether that college will serve as a tool to your professional future. You need to talk to staff in the department, whether a professor or dean's secretary, to learn about the school's internship network.

LOCATION

Location is another factor. As I will say in my section on social relationships, I recommend colleges that are either in cities or rural areas, not the suburbs. Cities offer a diversity of opportunities, such as museums, concerts, and libraries, as well as other conveniences such as eating establishments—i.e. you are not confined to campus food. There is also public transportation (in most cities, but not all), which precludes the need for a car and reduces accidents and expenses. Cities also have a number of other universities that will have guest lecturers and events.

Colleges in the countryside have the advantage of being relatively self-sufficient. They aim to have everything you may need, and have a deeper sense of community and camaraderie. Such colleges do not have as many distractions as colleges in the city, and are—at least on paper—safer. (That being said, crime happens everywhere.) Rural colleges also tend to arrange trips off campus, usually to a nearby city. Another nice aspect is that the townspeople are often very friendly to the college's students, as their businesses depend on them.

Lastly, there are the colleges in the suburbs, particularly the affluent suburbs of major cities such as Boston or Philadelphia. I caution against going to these suburban institutions. The residents of upscale towns are often unfriendly to college students, or at least unwelcoming, as they perceive students as troublemakers, and hence the police are overbearingly vigilant and strict. The schools themselves are not always self-sufficient, and because public transportation is rare, it becomes problematic to get around. There is also generally a very high level of social conformity—you will see that most of the students at these types of colleges dress and act the same.

Going to a college where everyone dresses like you and talks like you does not broaden your social horizons.

The latter remark relates to another aspect of college life that is important. Going to a college where everyone dresses like you and talks like you does not broaden your social horizons. Part of the function of college is giving you exposure to other kinds of people. This is not an attack on colleges that are mostly one race or religion. What I am advocating is diversity of thought. In your working life, you will deal with people of different backgrounds as well as different ways of thinking. Expose yourself to it so you can understand different people better.

CLASS SIZE AND PROFESSORS

College professors are a different breed than high school teachers. Many college professors are there for research, rather than teaching *per se*, and as they don't go through required teacher training, their styles can be tough to get used to. Some are absolutely brilliant, and others are little help at all. In short, they run the full spectrum.

Smaller class sizes at least give you a better chance of getting to know your professor better. Contrary to popular belief, it is not only the private colleges that have small class sizes. A list from 2016, published on www.collegeraptor.com, contains quite a number of large state schools with class sizes of fifteen students or less. And a class size of 20–25 still offers you plenty of opportunity to get to know your instructor. The site www.ratemyprofessors.com can shed some light on what students think of their professors.

In my experience, any professor who had Office Hours—which was all of them—was fair game for being pumped for information, and hence it didn't matter much how large the class size was. Anytime you have an assignment, the best thing to do is to go to that professor's office and ask a few questions. Once the professor gets talking, he often tells you the angle that he is looking for, or what he wants people to emphasize. If there is a test coming up, the professor will likely tell you what to focus on as preparation.

Weather

I personally did not like very hot weather when I was a college student, and would have found the South and Southwest to be unbearable. I suspect that most others are the opposite, and prefer to avoid cold weather. Just be mindful, if you are from the North, that colleges in climates of perpetual sunshine are often difficult places to focus on one's studies. There is always something fun to do outside, whether it involves throwing a ball around, swimming, or people-watching. Weather is something that we cannot change, so it pays to make sure you attend a college where the weather is conducive to your studying.

Distance

Some of us have no option but to go to a college that is quite far away from home. However, if you have the choice between two nearly identical schools, and one is quite far away, choose the one that is closer. One of my friends was given a "four-hour rule" by his parents when he was choosing a college: it had to be within four hours' driving distance. I would recommend avoiding the need to fly, unless the college is really offering something special. Plane flights are an annoyance. Of course, a college that you can reach by train is ideal.

Transferring

If you have given yourself six months at a college, and absolutely dislike the experience that you have had there, by all means think seriously about transferring elsewhere. This means evaluating the campus culture, the teachers and courses, and other aspects mentioned above. Don't be deceived into a misguided loyalty to stay. After all, it is your money that you are spending. Each semester, you are giving the college repeat business. So make sure they are making you a satisfied customer. I've never met anyone who transferred and regretted the decision.

6 Gap Years: And Avoiding Trap Years

Gap Years have become increasingly popular in the past two decades. In my time in Asia, I met literally thousands of people on their gap years, and have kept in touch with many of them long afterwards. While many spent their gap year working, usually teaching English, I also met quite a few who were just traveling. Their feedback as to the benefits of gap years, whether they worked or traveled, is very similar.

"Trap" Years

Gap years are to be handled with care and caution. The main reason is that gap years have a tendency to become "trap" years. Many people do gap years out of desperation, i.e. because they don't know what to do after college. In many cases, this is because they have studied an impractical major, and realize in their final semester that they are about to enter the ranks of the unemployed. Choosing to travel or to teach abroad

Gap years have a tendency to become "trap" years.

sounds better than planning to move back in with Mom and Dad and search for a job in sectors that aren't hiring.

Students then pass an enjoyable gap year, but as the gap year is ending, they see that they are in the same employment situation as when they started. With no prospects back home, the easiest thing to do is simple: another gap year. This cycle repeats itself at the end of that second year. After a few years, this individual—now 26 or 27—feels trapped, unable to try to start a regular career back home. At the same time, gap-year jobs such as teaching English do not pay a First World salary, so he is not earning enough to support a long-term financial future, which involves savings, investments, and owning property. Going back to the U.S. then becomes harder and harder each year.

"IF IT HASN'T HAPPENED IN THE U.S. . . ."

Despite what organizations that facilitate gap years will tell you, a gap year has little value to employers. Unfortunately, the general attitude of employers in the U.S. towards jobs abroad is, "If it hasn't happened in the U.S., then it hasn't happened." I think their view is narrow-minded, but this is what you will be up against. Employers have little interest in what you have done abroad, and while they may appreciate your cultural experience on a personal level, it is not enough to get you a job. Don't kid yourself that teaching English abroad will give you highly employable skills in the eyes of a U.S. employer. It actually won't even get you an English-teaching job in the U.S., as there are special degrees required for that.

Furthermore, interviewers like to be able to check references and companies, and find it difficult to check small firms in remote parts of the world. They are also suspicious of non-American companies. Hence, that school you taught at in South America, Europe, Asia, or Africa may not be taken seriously on your résumé.

One conclusion to be drawn here is that professionally it doesn't really matter what you do with your gap year. Whether you spend it visiting 25 countries, or just living in one, the overall effect is the same. Teaching English will help with your confidence in public speaking and awareness of a new culture. Traveling will enhance your logistical planning skills and expose you to greater diversity. Aside from that, it is a year of recreation, and employers know it.

How to Safely Do a Gap Year

I am often asked by young people when they should take their gap year, specifically whether to do it before college or after. My recommendation is to do it before your first year of college. This way, you have a definite plan as to what you will be doing when your gap year ends. It is also easier to go from a gap year to college than it is to go from a gap year to the harsher realities of the working world.

Students who want to go on a gap year after college should only do so if they already have a definite plan for when they come back. This can be a job that they have already secured, or a course, e.g. a Master's degree, that they have already researched and been accepted in. Naturally this degree should be in a practical subject.

If you have such a great gap year that you feel you must do another, make sure that you have an exact plan for what to do at the end of that second year. Otherwise, you are trapped. Limit yourself to two gap years at the most. Otherwise, you are falling behind your peers professionally, which will affect you on social and psychological levels, as well as financially.

PART TWO

7 Physical Health: Staying Strong and Slim

Some of the best advice I received before going to college pertained to physical health. Far too many college students neglect their health during these years, which are as formative to the body as to the mind. Many doctors and nutritionists would agree that the years 15–23 represent the peak of a human's physical aptitude. Furthermore, staying in shape during these years, and building a strong body, will stay with you throughout your life.

Exercise

One option is to play a sport. However, if you are just looking to maintain a decent level of physical health, playing a sport in college is overkill. Sports in college are a huge commitment: they require formal practice sessions every day, for long hours, and they become a lifestyle. While you grow close with your teammates, the confining lifestyle prevents you from engaging in other pursuits and meeting new people.

I myself did Crew during my freshman year, and ended up regretting it. Crew involved daily practices of three hours, beginning at 4:30 in the morning. While my friends and classmates were getting a decent night's sleep, and preparing for classes, I was running through the streets of Philadelphia and getting exhausted even before I started my academic day.

(Yes, Crew involves mostly running, with occasionally getting into the actual boats. The whole strategy is to trim the body down so it is at its lightest when one gets into the boats. One may as well just join the cross-country team!)

Other sports involve a similar time commitment. For compulsive jocks, who cannot live without playing sports and the thrill of competition, this is fine, but for most of us, it is not necessary to do a six-day-a-week sport to stay in shape. Simply going to the gym three times a week, doing some cardiovascular work on the treadmill and pumping some iron, will provide you with the muscular activity your body needs.

Please keep in mind that this does not mean just going through the motions. If you are using the exercise bike, go fast. If you are jogging, push yourself to go faster and longer. In short, if you are not sweating, and not gasping for breath at the end, you are not exercising hard enough.

For both men and women, I recommend an exercise regimen that focuses on the core muscles.

For both men and women, I recommend an exercise

regimen that focuses on the core muscles, especially the abdominals. I can think of no other muscle group that is as important. Leg exercises, particularly running, are also essential. For males, some attention should be paid to putting on mass in the chest and shoulders, to give a strong appearance. (Too many males just focus on building their upper arms.) An impressive physique will be helpful in many ways in life, both professionally and personally. To make things more measurable, I prescribe that every male should be able to bench press at least 200 pounds.

DIET

College students are notorious for poor eating habits. Most famously, there is the "Freshman 15," the 15 pounds of flab added during freshman year as a result of beer and late-night pizzas, and also due to the all-you-can-eat desserts in the dining hall. But aside from the Freshman 15, students fall into an atrocious diet of eating at the wrong times and not eating nutritiously.

While males certainly pack on the pounds, it seems that women are affected even more so by poor eating habits at this time of life. I went to the gym at 7 a.m. during college, and would see female classmates on the exercise bikes. Seeing them week after week over the course of a few years, I wondered why many of them weren't losing weight. As

Two-thirds of weight loss is directly related to one's diet.

I became closer friends with some of them, I found out: Two-thirds of weight loss is directly related to one's diet, and these young women were not eating properly. They skipped breakfast, and then had a salad at lunch, the positive effects of which they negated by loading it with salad dressing. At dinner, they ate sparingly. However, around 9pm—as a result of not eating much all day—they were ravenously hungry, and started attacking the desserts: ice cream, brownies, cake, potato chips, etc. In short, they indulged all the stuff that makes one gain weight. They felt justified in their self-indulgence, as they hadn't eaten all day. If they had eaten the right foods at the right times, they would not have been hungry.

So what is a balanced diet? Breakfast should contain some form of fruit or vegetable, as should lunch. Both meals should contain protein and carbohydrates. People who are looking to lose weight should not eat carbohydrates after 4pm. If you find yourself hungry in the late evening, drinking water will help, though for solid sustenance, eat cucumbers or celery. These add minimal, if any, calories. Bear in mind also that anything with sugar will make you put on weight. Soft drinks should be avoided at all costs, and in my opinion, should not even be made available in the dining halls.

While most males may not have the degree of "sweet-tooth" shared by their female counterparts, they do have a fondness for beer. Confine your beer-guzzling to weekends. There's nothing attractive about having a beer belly at 19 years old. I'll talk more about self-discipline in a succeeding chapter.

SLEEP

Getting proper sleep during your college years is a challenge, and one that requires proactive attention. You are up against dormitory life and living amongst people who have different schedules and priorities. While it may be fun to experience the late-night frivolity of dorm life during your first few weeks, you will quickly discover that waking up tired is not a way to go through life or to be productive. College is an exacting time of your life, in so many ways, and to handle it successfully, a stable sleeping schedule is essential.

> ***You should aim to get eight hours of sleep per night.***

You should aim to get eight hours of sleep per night. True, we can get by with six or seven, but has "getting by" ever resulted in anything worthwhile? An afternoon nap of 30–45 minutes is helpful, but you should treat it as an occasional luxury, not something you depend on. Afternoon naps will not be an option after graduation (unfortunately!).

You will also meet people who look tired all the time. And that's because they *are*. Far too many students allow themselves to fall into chronically poor sleeping habits, and it starts to affect the way they look. On top of that, these are the people who are constantly sick and missing out on classes and other elements of campus life.

Plenty of students get sick for long periods of time, due to living in close quarters. Keeping yourself well-rested, well-fed, and well-exercised is the best way to build up your defenses and prevent getting ill.

Those three subtopics sum it up. Taking care of your physical health requires basic attention to exercise, diet, and sleep. It's not complicated, and anyone can do it. So don't cheat yourself when it comes to your health, and never take it for granted.

Don't cheat yourself when it comes to your health, and never take it for granted.

8 Mental Health: Staying Positive and Fighting Anxiety

I've never met a successful person who was negative, and college is a critical time to examine one's level of positivity. Ask yourself the classic question, "Do I see the glass half empty or half full?" It is tempting, during these very intellectual years of one's life, to adopt an attitude of being very "realistic," i.e. using your knowledge to be critical and point out where things are deficient. This approach leads to an overall perspective of negativity, and finally, depression.

While depression can begin in high school, it is not uncommon for the first seeds of depression to sprout during one's college years. Unfortunately, in college, depression can be very difficult to self-diagnose. Depression generally involves a withdrawal from the world, a self-isolation, which is nearly impossible to do in a college environment, especially if one lives in a dormitory. College also keeps one busy enough with time-sensitive assignments, and periods of evaluation, such that one is forced to focus.

Nevertheless, the main sign to look for is a general negativity. Disliking all of your courses, not wishing to meet new people or get involved in campus life, and also being cynical. In addition to how you think about your life, pay attention to how you talk about yourself and about what is around you. As preacher Joel Osteen says, "Your words can trap you. What you say can cause you to stumble and keep you from your potential. You're not snared by what you think. Negative thoughts come to us all. But when you speak them out loud, you give them life. That's when they become a reality." He adds, "In other words, you can't talk negative and expect to live a positive life. You can't talk defeat and expect to have victory."

Pay attention to how you talk about yourself and about what is around you.

Finally, we are all born with the capacity to be positive. To go back to "the glass half-empty or half-full" scenario, being positive is a *choice*. And so is being negative. If you choose to see that glass half full, if you choose to be positive, happiness will be a part of your life. There's no such thing as being happy every minute of every day, but happiness will be something that you feel often, as long as you make the decision to be a positive person. For the negativist, happiness will be elusive, and ultimately, unattainable.

The "Attitude of Gratitude"

How can you start being positive? College students should take a moment each day to be thankful for all of the positive things in their lives. Too many people this age take good things for granted. For one, be thankful to be attending college—for having the cerebral, physical, and financial means to even be there. Be thankful for a family that supports you, for teachers who want to educate you, for an institution which is providing you with a trajectory to a prosperous future (as long as you choose the right major!). But don't confine your thankfulness to college: think of all the positive things in your life—good food, beautiful music, your hobbies, your friends, your health—the things you like and cherish. Never take any good thing for granted. Keep the "Attitude of Gratitude."

Anytime you are feeling unlucky or that others are better off than you, just think of all the tremendously bad things that could have happened to you today, but didn't. Fortune doesn't always *give*. Sometimes it just *prevents*.

Fortune doesn't always give. Sometimes it just prevents.

Anxiety

College is also an opportune time to assess whether you have anxiety issues. These will have already been present, if not noticed. In my case, I began to show evidence of an anxiety problem in elementary school. Anxiety as a disorder can be difficult to diagnose in scholastic environments, as the constant pressure of assignments and exams gives an excuse for stress. It is indeed reasonable to feel some stress, but what should be looked at is the worrying. If assignments fill you with worry, so much that you cannot stop thinking about them, and if your mind makes no distinction between small matters (seeing if a book you need is in the library) and large ones (getting an A on the final exam), you may very likely be an anxiety sufferer.

So what can you do about it? For one, you want to look at your daily life and make sure that you are living as physically healthy as possible. Bodily strength is important in fighting anxiety. If you drink alcohol, drink very moderately or not at all. A hangover combined with anxiety is a harsh combination. Get regular physical exercise that involves little time to think. I always believe that the benefits of exercise are 50% mental. The less you think, the less anxiety you feel. A class of cardiovascular exercises works wonders, or just running a few sprints on the treadmill. (I caution against very long runs—I think the brain adjusts and then starts thinking too deeply.) Take a look at your diet: make sure you are eating foods that will not put on weight, as you don't want to add your appearance to the things that are causing you anxiety.

Bodily strength is important in fighting anxiety.

One way to combat anxiety is to break everything down into parts. It is normal to feel overwhelmed when you receive a project or long-term assignment, such as a term paper: Finding the research materials, doing all the reading, taking notes, writing the paper—and this, in addition to all your other work. Break it down into parts: think of it not as a whole, but as a series of small, manageable steps. It takes more than one battle to win a war, and it takes more than one step to finish any worthwhile project in life.

One way to combat anxiety is to break everything down into parts.

One further aid against anxiety is the ability to compartmentalize. This approach involves mentally filing your urgencies to be focused on at a distinct time. While it is not easy skill to cultivate, it can indeed be done, with practice. CEOs and politicians are known for possessing this quality. The key to mastering it lies in your sense of confidence. Have you succeeded in accomplishing assignments in the past? Yes. Have you made it to college? Yes. Do you work hard, and do your best? Yes and yes. Hence, you don't need to focus on everything at one time. You know that when you get to it, at a time you have appointed for yourself, you will do it—and will do it well.

As always, I am strongly against the use of drugs to combat anxiety and depression. Contemporary psychiatry is far too generous in its recommendations for drug use. The result is young people becoming dependent on pills and experiencing serious side effects, both during active use and withdrawal.

I'd like to conclude this section with some suggested professions for those who suffer from anxiety disorder. Carefully managed, anxiety can be part of an otherwise peaceful and satisfying life. At the same time, there are jobs that suit people who are anxiety-prone, and jobs they should avoid. In general, the most control you have in a job—i.e. the less dependent you are on the decisions of other people—the more appropriate the job is for the anxiety sufferer. This rules out any Sales job. It also rules out a job where you are directly dealing with the stock market, as history shows there is no predictability there whatsoever. Jobs that require constant creativity, the need to reinvent the wheel every day, can also be problematic (such as advertising). Event-planning would also be ruled out.

Jobs which suit those who suffer from routine anxiety include:

- Doctor (non-surgical)
- College professor
- Accountant
- Quality control positions

- Operations Manager
- Many IT jobs also are very knowledge-based and allow you to work in your own sphere

These occupations fall into the classification of being knowledge-based. For many of them, having an anxiety condition can actually be helpful.

AVOIDING PERFECTIONISM

Perfectionism combines dangerously with anxiety. While it is noble to aim high, understand that perfection is not for us mere mortals. Notice that the U.S. Army says "Be all that you can be," not "Be perfect." You will make mistakes—it is part of life. In fact, a fear of making mistakes will impede your progress and actually result in you achieving LESS. As psychologist Tal Ben-Shahar states, "Perfectionism means paralysis."

A fear of making mistakes will impede your progress and actually result in you achieving LESS.

Never expect your life to run perfectly. It took me till my mid-30s to accept that "shit happens." Learn this at an early age—that there are unfortunate things that happen over which we have no control. All we can do is deal with them in the most serene and practical manner possible, and learn and grow from them. One line I always remember from the ***Imitation of Christ*** is, "In temptations and troubles a man is proved."

This acceptance of imperfection also applies to other people. We often subconsciously deny that the human race is imperfect, and that hence there are plenty of difficult people to deal with. Roman emperor Marcus Aurelius, in his ***Meditations***, even suggests, "Begin the morning by saying to thyself, I shall meet with the busybody, the ungrateful, arrogant, deceitful, envious, unsocial." In other words, don't be surprised when you meet people who are difficult. An imperfect world means that perfection is just not part of the human condition.

THE PAST

As human beings, it is common for us to think about the past, and unfortunately, we tend to dwell on our mistakes. German self-help writer Eckhart Tolle begins his classic book ***The Power of Now*** by saying, "I have little use for the past and rarely think about it." This is the approach to the past that you must take, if you want to move forward. We have all made mistakes in our pasts—social, academic, personal mistakes—and we learn what we can from them, and then must avoid thinking about them.

Those who continue thinking about the past will continue to relive it.

Those who continue thinking about the past will continue to relive it. But there is no reason to obsess about the past. It is a trap, which can be addictive.

Ignoring the past is an important skill to learn at an early age. If you are prone to dwelling on the past, make a habit of "catching" yourself when you are thinking about it, and reminding yourself how useless the past really is. Simply tell yourself to "change the channel." You are where you are at this moment, and regardless of what mistakes or triumphs you have experienced, you are at another beginning. Every day has the potential for progress, and every day is an opportunity to improve yourself.

The Future

Your approach to the future should be slightly different. We must always be attuned to the present, as the present is where our decisions are made. At the same time, we need to be attentive to the future. College is not all about being mentally in the present. It is a springboard, a trajectory, for your future place in life. Your college years are one of the few times of life where your future is almost as important as your present.

True, in life we will always have goals, which represent the future. But we don't need to think about them constantly, or we will lose our grasp of the present. College requires you to keep the future in mind a bit more, as you are spending four years that have a disproportionately heavy influence on the rest of your life. Your major, your learning, the social skills that you develop—these will all be applicable to each day of your post-college experience.

You will hear people say, "Live every day as if it is your last," though this notion is absurd, unless you are very old or terminally ill. However, to divide your life between past and future is to die in the present. One can never hold the future in one's hand. It is constantly in motion. Keep your mind in the present, with the understanding that what you do today has a strong influence on your tomorrow.

To divide your life between past and future is to die in the present.

9 Relationships: Parental, Romantic, Social, and Spiritual

I'd like to start my discussion of different kinds of relationships with the timeless adage, "Do unto others as you would have them do unto you." It is one of the simplest pieces of advice on human interaction ever given, though many people choose to ignore it. For those who master it, and make it part of their character, a world of fulfilling and rewarding relationships awaits.

So let's take a look at the different relationships you will have at this period of your life: parental, romantic, social, and spiritual.

Parental

Mark Twain once wrote, "When I was a boy of 14, my father was so ignorant I could hardly stand to have the old man around. But when I got to be 21, I was astonished at how much the old man had learned in seven years." We start to judge our parents when we reach our teens, and unfortunately we have a very limited perspective.

Overall, high school will try your relationship with your parents like no other time in your life. While you are contending for independence, your parents are trying to maintain control over your life, out of concern for your future. Your exposure to more of society, and the pros and cons that it brings, weakens their influence over you. On top of that, there is your academic stress, particularly during Junior Year.

Much of this stress comes from wanting to get into a "good" college, though as I have said earlier, most of the colleges available are good, and your direction—your choice of major and career—is more important than the college that you go to.

You will find that high school pressure abates after you take your SATs in the autumn of Senior Year. This is a time for celebration (but not "Senioritis"!). The test that has haunted you for years has now been taken for the last time; you have done your absolute best; and you can now relax somewhat. You are halfway through the first semester and can keep your grades up, though you no longer have the SAT thorn in your side, and meanwhile you are sending off your college applications. In addition to being a time to de-stress, it is a time to work on your relationship with your parents, and to dress any wounds.

In the words of Samuel Johnson, "Parents we can have but once." Spend more time with them, for you will be going away on a long-term basis. Get to know them, for life will not give you such an easy opportunity again. Make sure to be on good terms with them when you leave. It is difficult to repair a relationship from afar.

The Parental Visit

When you are at college, don't deny your parents a weekly chat on the phone. Try to put yourself in their shoes: they have spent every day with you for 18 years, raising and caring for you, and you have been the main focus of their lives. You are more important, more precious to them, than you realize. It is tempting to think that you are now independent and want to distance yourself from your parents. But don't distance yourself personally in addition to geographically.

Don't deny your parents a weekly chat on the phone.

Sometime during Freshman Year, often called Parents Weekend, your parents will come to college to see you. Alternatively, they may just come on their own. While there is that temptation for you to accentuate your independence, choose a course which shows that you are capable of independence but also appreciate their visit. These are the people who have helped get you here, and who are probably paying for it. Treat your parents like visiting ambassadors. Take them out to dinner and pay for the meal. Take them to a football game. Don't be hung-over. Dress well. Don't spend the time complaining about your courses or your dorm. Show them the fine, mature adult that you are becoming. At the same time, you will also find your parents more relaxed towards you.

This is a pivotal time to establish a positive, harmonious relationship. Like it or not, your relationship with Mom and Dad will be important for many years, no matter how financially independent you become. Your parents will be crucial advisors when you are out in the world and looking to do such things as buy a house, get insurance, and raise children. Parenting never ends, and the nice thing is that most parents never want it to.

Never forget that your parents' primary concern is to see you happy. Yes, they want you to be successful, but even the strictest and most ambitious parents believe that their child's happiness is paramount. These are the people who love you more than you can possibly understand—and which you *won't* understand till you have kids of your own. Keep this in mind when they bombard you with daily phone calls during your first semester. For 18 years, you have been their world.

ROMANTIC

Naturally it is difficult to tell someone how to live one's love life. However, in this section I would like to give some advice that helps you avoid spending a great deal of emotional energy and time that could instead be used on strengthening your foundation for the future.

Long-distance Relationships

In your freshman year of college, you will see that many fellow classmates are still involved in relationships with their girlfriends or boyfriends from high school. Typically these involve weekend visits, either to back home or other colleges, and quite a lot of time spent chatting online and on the phone. While there is something noble about trying to make a relationship work over distances, I must say that I have never seen a long-distance relationship last beyond freshman year. In the second semester, the emotional phone calls begin, jealousy on both sides kicks in, and the inevitable solution to break up is eventually proposed.

Long-distance relationships also restrict your integration into college life, making you reluctant to join groups and keeping you away from socializing with other students on weekends.

Moderation and Understanding

On-campus relationships are much more common, and are easier. If you do decide to have a relationship, beware of confining all of your free time to it. Make sure to have other friends and other interests. The classic case is the couple who date intensely for two or three years and then break up just before senior year. Each partner then realizes that they haven't invested

If you do decide to have a relationship, beware of confining all of your free time to it.

much time in other friendships, and have no friends or social lives. In short, make sure that your relationship is not the only aspect of your social life.

Within amatory relationships, I recommend that you and your "significant other" both read John Gray's ***Men Are from Mars, Women Are from Venus***. This is the best book about gaining mutual understanding between the sexes. It presents excellent insights, such as how women need a man to be a good listener, and how men need time for solitude when dealing with a problem. Despite all the advances made in making men and women equal in the eyes of the law (advances that I applaud), the two sexes remain very different emotionally and psychologically.

SOCIAL

College is the ideal time for developing your social skills, to become the person who will have strong interpersonal abilities in the adult and working world. Despite living in an age of digital technology, these skills remain extremely important: regardless of how technically skilled and knowledgeable you are, companies will only hire you if they think they can get along with you.

> ***College is the ideal time for developing your social skills.***

Developing strong interpersonal skills is easier than one thinks. I went to college as a shy young man who wanted to keep his distance, and I emerged into the working world as someone who was gregarious and had a deep appreciation for friendship. One of the reasons for this was that the people you meet in college are simply *nicer* than the ones you've met before. Like yourself, your fellow students have matured through high school, through age and experience, and overall treat people better.

So how to develop one's interpersonal skills? First, politeness plays a huge role in how well one is liked. Being polite costs nothing, it is easy, and it makes a huge difference. Another quality that attracts people is positivity. Those who are negative and cynical will attract few friends; worse off, they will attract other people who are also cynical and negative, creating a collective downward spiral. Positive people are enjoyable to be around. This does not mean that you have to be loud or even bubbly. Just keeping an overall positive mentality, and a cheerful disposition, is enough.

Getting Involved

One question I am often asked by prospective college students is, "Should I join a fraternity?" (Naturally, young women ask if they should join a sorority.) Greek life has its pros and cons, so bear in mind that there is no clear-cut, perfect decision. For the purposes of this discussion, I will use "fraternity" to represent both, as the same advice applies equally.

If your college is in a rural area, you will quickly find that the social life is limited. This is where fraternity life is valuable. Fraternities have an organized structure that provides for social outings, activities, and the formation of friendships. If you are in a rural college, e.g. somewhere in Pennsylvania or upstate New York, joining a fraternity will be your easiest way of having an active social life.

For those going to college in the city, the decision is a bit more complicated. A metropolis, like New York City, offers such a multitude of diversions that a fraternity is not necessary for creating social opportunities. The more interests and hobbies you have, the more you will find that there are plenty of groups dedicated to these pursuits, and that these groups have their own social functions. For smaller cities, or cities in quieter and more conservative parts of the country, you may want to join a fraternity, as again, you will not be able to depend on your city alone for a social life.

As mentioned earlier, the third type of college location is the suburbs. My college had Greek life, though activities—especially parties—were restricted to off-campus. Still, I can safely say that at a suburban college, joining the Greek system is a big plus. Without the Greek system, life at a suburban college can be rather boring. The town itself will consist of middle-class or affluent families who consider the college students to be a nuisance, and hence the police pay a lot of attention to students' carousing. Secondly, students become reliant on trips to "the city" to have fun, and this is not convenient. You don't want to have to drive miles and miles every time you want a night out. If you are 50/50 about joining a fraternity, my advice is to join one.

Moving away from fraternities and sororities, there are lots of other ways in college to get involved and develop your social skills. My recommendation is to try as many things as you can during freshman year. I have already cautioned about joining organized sports teams, but otherwise, you will find that most clubs and organizations are not particularly rigorous. Joining different clubs is an easy way of amassing a large number of friends and acquaintances, which also comes in handy if you decide to run for any student government positions. To make some friends from backgrounds other than your own, try joining a club that is on the fringes of your interests. You'll learn more about people, which is one of the benefits to be derived from the college experience.

Joining different clubs is an easy way of amassing a large number of friends and acquaintances.

Whatever you do, don't let your college life be divided only between the classroom and the dorm. No matter how introverted you are, force yourself to have a social life, even if it is just one club. Otherwise, you are missing out on a critical opportunity to develop much-needed social skills.

One final word of advice: in this digital age, so much of our socializing takes place over social media. Be careful about what you post. Don't put anything online that would jeopardize you being hired by a future employer. Regretfully, we live in a judgmental age, and with all the technology available, it is not difficult to get a lot of information on someone's life with just a few taps on the keyboard. People, including employers, will judge you partly by your Facebook page, so keep it as inoffensive as possible.

Don't put anything online that would jeopardize you being hired by a future employer.

SPIRITUAL

Part of our passage into adulthood involves recognizing the fact that happiness is not something we achieve alone. Life has too many burdens to bear without a sense of purpose, of meaning, and of heaving another element there for support. This is where the spiritual side of life comes in. It acts as both a motivator and a comfort.

Many of us are raised in households that are at least somewhat religious; for example, many of us will have had to attend church on Sunday with our parents. We then go through a period of teen rebellion, where we spurn what our parents tried to enforce.

College is a time to reexamine the role of spirituality in your life.

College is a time to reexamine the role of spirituality in your life—to view it not as an imposition from your parents or other authorities, but as something from which you can derive peace, fulfillment, and confidence.

It comes as a great comfort to know that there is a being who wants you to be happy and wants to give you strength. I was very nonchalant in my attitude towards God until I needed him, and when I turned to him, in desperation, and asked for help, I felt a surge of strength. The more I believed in God, the stronger I felt. God is not a "genie," he does not give material gifts, but his gifts come in spiritual form.

Having worked with people who also have a strong spiritual side, I have seen that they are generally more upbeat about facing each day, and psychologically much better at handling life's misfortunes. All of them exemplify the "attitude of gratitude" that I mentioned earlier. In fact, many of these individuals begin their day with a prayer, or even some form of meditation.

Taking 20 minutes each day to "regroup," to enjoy silence and stillness, is essential to maintaining peace of mind, as well as a balanced perspective on life. It helps us to avoid getting carried away with the exigencies of the mundane world. So often, the goings-on around us build up into a momentum that feels irresistible; we find ourselves caught up in a whirlwind, and we lose our footing. But we should know that this whirlwind is escapable. College campuses have plenty of space for early morning walks, and they of course have a library, where you can get that 20–30 minutes of stillness.

An excellent book about appreciating stillness, about staying in the moment and not losing your footing, is Eckhart Tolle's ***The Power of Now***, which I mentioned earlier. The book tells us how to ignore the past, how to train our minds to focus, and how to enjoy the present. Similarly titled, another great book for spiritual development—more religious in nature—is Joel Osteen's ***The Power of I Am***. Osteen is a master at fusing together spirituality, God, and the self-help genre, and the result is very inspiring.

We often discover the spiritual side of ourselves when we need it most; but why wait till we experience adversity to learn how to deal with it?

10 Self-Discipline: Time, Money, and the Easy Things

College represents your first real trial of self-discipline. Never before have you had so little supervision and so much free time. The first few days are a mixture of euphoria and confusion, much like when we first learn to walk but don't know where to go. It is at this time that your notion of self-discipline becomes critical. I saw so many instances of above-average students failing during Freshman year, and in all cases, it boiled down to their inability for self-control and focus.

You will find dormitory life to be interesting, a bit claustrophobic, and full of distractions. After a few weeks, you will see a clear distinction between the night-owls and the early-birds. In the case of the night owls, they are generally staunch procrastinators, who finally bite the bullet at 2 a.m. to write a paper that is due that morning. Due to this type of schedule, they often miss classes and then have to rely on other students' notes.

This brings me to one of the most important pieces of advice that I can give, with regard to classes, which simply is: SHOW UP. So much of life involves being present, and 50% of any job consists of simply being there. Missing classes means that you miss information about upcoming tests, exams, papers, review sessions, and of course valuable notes, while of course also missing the opportunity to develop any rapport with the professor or other classmates. One of my professor friends has students—usually freshmen—who ask him on the first day how many classes they can miss. It is no coincidence that the students with this attitude are the ones who fail his course. I cannot imagine an easier way to fail than to not show up.

> ***50% of any job consists of simply being there.***

> ***I cannot imagine an easier way to fail than to not show up.***

MAKING THE MOST OF YOUR TIME

Marcus Aurelius, in his ***Meditations***, writes, "In the morning when you rise unwillingly, let this thought be present: I am rising to the work of a human being. Why, then, am I dissatisfied if I am going to do the things for which I exist, and for which I was brought into the world? Do you exist then just to take your pleasure, and not at all for action or exertion?" What Aurelius is emphasizing here, is that whatever our purpose in life may be, it is not to be lazy.

College students should get eight hours of sleep a night, with seven hours as the absolute minimum. This can be difficult, with the constant interruption of neighbors in your dormitory, but I suggest getting into bed at 11pm at the latest.

One thing that alarmed me, after my first few weeks as a freshman, was the sheer abundance of leisure time—or what appeared to be so. One upper-classman gave me advice about how to deal with this newfound abundance of hours: "In college, the *more* you do, the *better* you do." He was referring to extracurricular activities, such as clubs, charity organizations, and student government. Over the next four years, I was happy to observe that those who got the most involved were also those who had the strongest academic performance. Why? Because their busy schedules forced them to budget their time and use it judiciously. They did not fall into the trap of coming home from class and sitting idly in their dorms.

Incidentally, one of the biggest time-wasters during college is video games. My next-door neighbor in the dorm brought his video game system and collection (the old Nintendo) to his room after Thanksgiving break during freshman year, and I saw his room turn into a 24-hour arcade of people coming in—choosing their time to play, not leaving, and arguing about whose turn was next. There was a constant loud group in his small room, whether he was there or not, and at one point he stopped going there except to (try to) sleep. With all of the ways to enrich yourself during college, video games are the least productive of them all.

The other way to waste vast amounts of time is through indulgence in marijuana. While the remedial health factors continue to be debated, and its use re-legislated, it is clear that pot does not make one motivated or provide a lifestyle that is conducive to personal development. Habitual pot-smoking—and it almost always becomes habitual—involves a lot of late nights, an overall lackadaisical feeling, dressing like you just fell out of bed, and associating with people who, while they may be very nice individuals, are generally not very motivated. And college is certainly not a time to be unmotivated.

A NOTE ON ALCOHOL

Of course, I cannot give official approval for people to indulge in the under-age drinking of alcohol. However, I accept the reality that college students do it. (I did.) So if you are going to drink, you might as well know how to do it in a way that is safe and has minimal consequences.

The biggest mistake that college students make with alcohol involves hard liquor.

The biggest mistake that college students make with alcohol involves hard liquor. Their relative inexperience with hard liquor leads them to underestimate its strength, and they drink too much of it in too short a time period, often resulting in hospitalization and worse. In my freshman year, one of my dorm-mates drank 15 shots of vodka in less than half an hour. When he passed out and his face started turning blue, we had him rushed to the hospital. Apparently if we had waited any longer than we did, there would have been brain damage.

My advice with hard alcohol is simple: drink beer instead. Compared to its alcohol counterparts of beer and wine, hard liquor is the unhealthiest, is more expensive, and is the least predictable in its effects. Wine does not seem to be a popular choice among college students, partly because of its price per volume. Beer is somewhat predictable in its effects: we know what will happen, generally, if we have two beers or ten. Aside from the calories that it packs on, beer, in moderation, does not have serious side-effects for the average person.

This section would not be complete without a note concerning drunk driving. Naturally you have been told of the dangers of it for many years, but I would feel guilty if I did not reiterate some of it here. Simply put, there is never a reason to drive drunk. There is never anything so important that you need to get behind the wheel of a several-ton vehicle that will move at superhuman speed, without perfect control of your

Simply put, there is never a reason to drive drunk.

reflexes and decisions. If you have to think about whether you have had too much to drink, it means you have.

Before you arrive on campus for freshman year, take two $20 bills, fold them up, and stick them inside one of the sections of your wallet. This should be enough for two taxi rides or one long one. (And if you think you'd need more money, put more in your wallet.) I've known too many cases of people whose lives were destroyed by drunk driving. Getting caught by the police for DUI can also derail your path to success. Make it a cardinal rule of your life: never drink and drive.

The Easy Things

Fortunately, there are a number of qualities in life that require little or no talent to have, but which are still extremely impressive and valuable.

Things that require no inborn talent:

- Being punctual: many of us get into a habit of being late, not realizing how that is interpreted by other people—especially those who are always having to wait for us.

- Energy: getting a decent night's sleep, and staying hydrated, are not difficult to do. Nor is it difficult to put that energy into action.

- A positive attitude: as I've said before, being positive or negative is a choice.

- Doing more than is expected of you: going through life as a "minimalist" will not help you. Putting in a little extra effort yields rewards, and separates you from the competition.

- Being prepared: never trust that just "winging it" will achieve a good result. Remember the "Five P" rule: Proper preparation prevents poor performance.

- Politeness: "Good manners don't cost anything," as the old saying goes.

- A willingness to learn: Don't resent or be critical about the things you don't know. On the contrary, try to cram as much relevant knowledge as you can into your head now, as it gets harder to learn new things after 25.

Another quality that requires no innate aptitude is the simple philosophy of "Keep things moving forward." Say to yourself, each morning, that every day has the potential for progress.

GOALS

We have been told to have goals since elementary school. School defines our goals for us: getting an A on a test, for the quarter, semester, or year; winning awards; elevating our class rank. But life does not give us such clear and convenient gradations of measuring progress. Life makes them nebulous.

Goals are unclear when you are entering Freshman year, but they are easier to define when we put ourselves into the shoes of a college graduate. We want to be earning enough money to live independently, to have some savings and investments, and to have a comfortable lifestyle. We've already covered this numerically with the minimum salary threshold.

And what about our other goals? Professionally, salary should not be your only goal. You want to keep moving forward with your career—making more achievements, getting more recognition. In today's environment, constant new achievements are required of employees. Fortunately or unfortunately, the world is moving so fast that we have little time to sit around procrastinating; we are forced to achieve things each day. What is important is to avoid complacency. If you don't aim high, there are plenty of other people who will, and they will surpass you. Without goals, life becomes stagnant and boring, and once a job becomes boring, you start to resent having to do it. Things only get worse from there.

If you don't aim high, there are plenty of other people who will.

While getting A's is nice, be careful not to burn yourself out. Those who put too much pressure on themselves to achieve the highest marks in the class often become exhausted and get sick of school. There will be more tests and qualifications after college: GREs, MCATs, GMATs, etc. If you burn yourself out in high school and college, you won't want to take these tests. Getting a B is not the worst thing in the world, especially if it allows you to keep your mental and physical health.

Managing Your Money

Few of us have a ton of spending-money during our college days. College is a time to learn frugality, even with the small amount of money we may have. There is something to be gained from every difficult experience, and an ability to save money will help you for the rest of your life.

An ability to save money will help you for the rest of your life.

My chief advice here is to only use cash for all purchases. You will probably have a lot of offers from credit card companies, whether online or through cold-calls (these companies somehow get the lists of freshmen's phone numbers), but I urge you to resist them. Credit cards have an insidious quality of "Pleasure now, Pain later", which is hard to resist once you have that magic plastic in your hand.

By all means, have a debit ATM card, but beware of credit cards. They have put many a college student into serious debt, often from just one night of reckless drunken spending, and have caused the need for him or her to make embarrassing phone calls to Mom and Dad for help—not exactly reinforcing the student's claim of having reached independence.

Credit cards are much more applicable for junior or senior year of college, when the novelty of college freedom has subsided, and when it is advisable to start building a credit history. The latter will be important for buying cars, renting apartments, and so forth.

Another money-saving tip is quite simple. Limit the number of nights that you go out socially. Once you are out, you lose control of spending, especially if you are in a group. Restrict the number of nights you go out to one or two a week. Unfortunately, the only way to definitely save money is to not go out.

Preparing for Lectures Beforehand

One way to be proactive and keep a steady momentum is to look over upcoming material before it is presented by your professor. This was a little trick I picked up as a result of having some teachers who frankly didn't teach well. Many of the classroom environments do not provide for the ease of intimate questioning that we have in high school, and for the more technical or complex courses, I started taking a close look at the lesson on the night before the class, and making note of any questions. This way, during the class, my mind was not starting from scratch to wrap its head around the new idea or concept. When I did ask questions, professors were impressed that I seemed so familiar with the new material! Hence, it is a good idea to stay one step ahead of your professors.

11 Summer Breaks: A Weapon, Not a Waste

On the day that I returned to campus for sophomore year, I sat down for lunch with my roommate and his father. The first thing his father said was, "You boys need to start thinking about what you want to do next summer."

His advice came as quite a shock to me, as next summer was ten months away. But also, I had always thought that summer was a time to recover from the stress and burdens of schoolwork, to have fun, and to earn a little money which I could then spend during the next year of classes.

My friend's dad was really saying that summer was a time to significantly augment your education and employability—not three months that were a vacuum for both. During these great years for mental fecundity, ages 15–23, there should never be a three-month period where learning totally stops. (Nor should there be such a period in the rest of your life, either.)

I realize that for many of us, working during the summer is not a "choice," but a necessity. If so, try to find work that is at least relatable to your choice of career. Colleges, as mentioned, should be able to introduce you to many internship opportunities with prominent companies, or else those colleges aren't worth attending. If you have a job that is unrelated to your major and career, but not too rigorous, see if you can also work part-time on an unpaid basis with a company that is in your field. The ideal situation is a paid internship, though these are hard to find. The point is to start preparing for your summer break long before summer begins. Don't wait till the day after final exams have finished.

Start preparing for your summer break long before summer begins.

Everyone should try a sales job once during their summer breaks. Being in sales, as I have said earlier, is no picnic, but it is good for you to see what business is like on the front lines. Three months of doing front-line sales will be enough to alienate you from it for life, while also giving you a first-hand look at customer behavior. It will also help you learn certain skills, including empathy and persuasiveness. Sales jobs are not difficult to find: companies are always hiring salespeople, as salespeople are always leaving or getting fired!

Aside from jobs, summer is also an excellent time for self-directed learning. For the cost of $25, you can take an online course in your field from companies like Udemy, perhaps even one that prepares you for your upcoming year of study. For the last time in this book, your mind is at its most fertile during the ages of 15–23, so why not make the most of it? You can start learning a language, take a course on personal financial investments, or make improvements in your knowledge of your major—all from the comfort of your own home, and all for next to nothing in costs.

Summer is as well a great time for researching graduate schools and companies. This knowledge is at your fingertips. Find out the graduate schools that offer the best programs for you, and find out the best companies in your field.

Always make sure to read at least one book during summer break. You want your mind to stay in the habit of reading, and to stay active, not undergo atrophy. If you are going to limit yourself to only one book, make it one that is educative and challenging, not a book you can read inattentively on the beach. Here is a reading list:

Always make sure to read at least one book during summer break.

- ***The Autobiography of Benjamin Franklin***
- Napoleon Hill, ***Think and Grow Rich***
- Marcus Aurelius, ***Meditations***

- Eckhart Tolle, ***The Power of Now***
- John Gray, ***Men Are from Mars, Women Are from Venus***
- Seth Godin, ***All Marketers Are Liars***
- Dale Carnegie, ***How to Win Friends and Influence People***
- Robert Kiyosaki, ***Rich Dad, Poor Dad***
- Thomas Piketty, ***Capital in the Twenty-First Century***
- Benjamin Graham, ***The Intelligent Investor*** (the edition with chapter-by-chapter commentary by Jason Zweig)

For those who will be doing gap years, make this your reading list for that year abroad.

Parting Words

I'd like to end here with some words that will add a final dimension to what we've talked about. I hope you've found our journey together to be informative, challenging, and most of all, helpful. Thank you for giving me the opportunity to share the information and lessons which I truly believe will put you on the right track for college and beyond.

Don't Forget: Life Is Difficult

Psychologist M. Scott Peck begins his classic book ***The Road Less Traveled*** with the phrase, "Life is difficult." And he is right. Yet it is amazing to see how many people enter college and adulthood expecting life to be easy. In the thousands of years that humans have existed, many of our difficulties have not changed. Don't be deceived by technology, and the ease of such things as instantaneously downloading music and sending messages across the world. Life is still difficult. We still have to work in order to eat; relationships remain complicated by our human nature; we still get sick. And of course, we still die.

It is amazing to see how many people enter college and adulthood expecting life to be easy.

I have endeavored, in this book, to help you to learn things the easy way, so you don't have to learn them the hard way. In following my guidance, you will find life easier. I speak from experiences, both good and bad, and I hope you'll take my advice so you don't have to go through the bad ones personally. Believe me, you want to avoid a bad experience if you can!

At the height of the Roman Empire, the military scholar Vegetius Renatus wrote, "If you want peace, prepare for war." I often apply this maxim to our path through life. If we want a smooth and comfortable life—one that is relatively "peaceful"—we have to prepare for it as if we were preparing for war. This means having the financial, mental, physical, and other foundations that are necessary. Life may not be exactly "war," but it is full of conflicts, confrontations, and calamities. In short, it is full of challenges.

As with preparing for war, preparing for life is something to be taken very seriously. Choosing the wrong major slows down your preparation for the financial challenges of life. Failing to take care of yourself physically makes you weak for the times when life comes at you strong.

Altruism

In this book, I have talked about the path to success. But what to do with that success when you achieve it? Some of that is up to you: pursuing hobbies, raising a family. But one aspect which is often overlooked is using that success to help others.

Humans have puzzled for ages over the meaning of life, and as of 2017, we are not one step closer to knowing what it is. Nonetheless, I can assure you that whatever the meaning of life may be, it is certainly not to be selfish.

Whatever the meaning of life may be, it is certainly not to be selfish.

Never forget that every blessing carries with it a burden. With a higher position, comes more accountability; with marriage, comes a more complex life; with children, comes a great deal more responsibility. And with success, comes a social duty.

Your prosperity will bring with it the burdens of hard work, but there is another burden—that of your duty to be generous towards your fellow man. Those who are blessed financially have a responsibility to those who, for whatever reason, have not been as fortunate. The United States has been a meritocracy for so long that we are not prepared for an economy that inherently favors the wealthy. That economy, which some are calling Neo-feudalism, is on its way. Our country is experiencing a shrinking middle class, and we have a duty to make sure we do not develop the socioeconomic situation of

Third World countries, where a small rich elite makes the decisions—all of which are to their own benefit. In societies like these, crime is rampant, healthcare for the masses declines, public property is regularly destroyed, and education levels drop.

In the words of Rotary International, "We increase our standard of living, so we can increase our standard of *giving*." Be generous with your money to those who are in need. You'll find that the joy it brings you far exceeds whatever sums you give away.

The Little Things

Finally, I haven't outwardly stated that you should "enjoy" college, as I know you will. There's plenty to enjoy. Ironically, when graduates reminisce about their college days and think about what they miss, it's not the sports events or the parties. Rather, it is the little things: bumping into a friend on campus and just chatting for three hours; staying up till dawn to talk and solve the problems of the world; and having thousands of people around you who are the same age.

As with all of the enjoyable features of life, don't take these things for granted. Be thankful for them, and be thankful for the ability to see, to walk, to think, to hear. Each day has the potential for progress, and all of this is made possible by things we rarely take the time to be thankful for.

Make the most of every advantage you've been given. Take a moment, every day, to cherish and be thankful for your life. It's the only one you've got.

Made in the USA
Middletown, DE
03 December 2018